T0318953

Cambridge Elements ≡

Elements in Ancient Philosophy
edited by
James Warren
University of Cambridge

ARISTOTLE ON ONTOLOGICAL PRIORITY IN THE *CATEGORIES*

Ana Laura Edelhoff
University of Oxford

CAMBRIDGE
UNIVERSITY PRESS

CAMBRIDGE
UNIVERSITY PRESS

University Printing House, Cambridge CB2 8BS, United Kingdom

One Liberty Plaza, 20th Floor, New York, NY 10006, USA

477 Williamstown Road, Port Melbourne, VIC 3207, Australia

314–321, 3rd Floor, Plot 3, Splendor Forum, Jasola District Centre,
New Delhi – 110025, India

79 Anson Road, #06–04/06, Singapore 079906

Cambridge University Press is part of the University of Cambridge.

It furthers the University's mission by disseminating knowledge in the pursuit of education, learning, and research at the highest international levels of excellence.

www.cambridge.org
Information on this title: www.cambridge.org/9781108812726
DOI: 10.1017/9781108874243

First published 2020

A catalogue record for this publication is available from the British Library.

ISBN 978-1-108-81272-6 Paperback
ISSN 2631-4118 (online)
ISSN 2631-410X (print)

Aristotle on Ontological Priority in the *Categories*

Elements in Ancient Philosophy

DOI: 10.1017/9781108874243
First published online: October 2020

Ana Laura Edelhoff
University of Oxford

Author for correspondence: analaura.edelhoff@some.ox.ac.uk

Abstract: The main objective of this Element is to reconstruct Aristotle's view on the nature of ontological priority in the *Categories*. Over the last three decades, investigations into ontological dependence and priority have become a major concern in contemporary metaphysics. Many see Aristotle as the originator of these discussions and, as a consequence, there is considerable interest in his own account of ontological dependence. In light of the renewed interest in Aristotelian metaphysics, it will be worthwhile – both historically and systematically – to return to Aristotle himself and to see how he conceived of ontological priority (what he calls "priority in substance" (*proteron kata ousian*) or "priority in nature" (*proteron tēi phusei*)), which is to be understood as a form of asymmetric ontological dependence.

Keywords: ontological priority, ontological dependence, Aristotle, Categories, primary substances

ISBNs: 9781108812726 (PB), 9781108874243 (OC)
ISSNs: 2631-4118 (online), 2631-410X (print)

Contents

1 Introduction

1.1 What Is Ontological Priority?

Over the last three decades, investigations into ontological dependence and priority have become a major concern in contemporary metaphysics. Many see Aristotle as the originator of these discussions and, as a consequence, there is considerable interest in his own account of ontological dependence. For instance, Fabrice Correia writes:

> The use of notions of dependence goes back as far as Aristotle's fourfold classification of beings, where the distinction between (primary and secondary) substances and non-substances is indeed characterized by means of a concept of ontological (in)dependence (Correia, 2008: 1013).[1]

This recent interest in Aristotle is best seen as part of a general renaissance of Aristotelian metaphysics. Since the 1990s, Aristotelian metaphysics – including core Aristotelian ideas such as essentialism and hylomorphism – have become popular again.[2]

In light of the renewed interest in Aristotelian metaphysics, it will be worthwhile – both historically and systematically – to return to Aristotle himself and to see how he himself conceived of ontological priority (what he calls 'priority in substance' (*proteron kat' ousian*) or 'priority in nature' (*proteron tēi phusei*)),[3] which is to be understood as a form of asymmetric ontological dependence. In this Element, I intend to show that my analysis is of value not only as a historical reconstruction of Aristotle but also to philosophers who are currently working on these issues, given that Aristotle provides keen insights into and discussions of ontological dependence.

In order to understand what ontological dependence is and where it applies, it is helpful to consider the ways in which metaphysicians conceive the structure of reality. Some metaphysicians take reality to have a *flat structure*: everything has the same ontological status (= all entities are equally fundamental) and belongs to the same category (= class of being). Others claim that everything has the same ontological status but that there are different categories (e.g. objects, properties, events, etc.). We might call this take on reality a *sorted structure*. Others still claim that the things that exist can have a different

---

[1] Cf. Fine (1995: 270).

[2] Kit Fine's work has contributed most to this revival of Aristotelian metaphysics. See Fine, 1994a; 1994b; 1995; 2001. Strawson's *Individuals* (1959) can be seen as the first break from the then widely popular Quinean metaphysics.

[3] In the following, I will use the terms 'ontological priority', 'priority in nature', and 'priority in substance' interchangeably.

ontological status in addition to belonging to different categories (= *ordered structure*).[4]

According to Aristotelian metaphysics, reality is an ordered structure. It is the task of the metaphysician to study both what exists and what is fundamental.[5] For metaphysicians who take the world to have an ordered structure, understanding dependencies is a central task.

An entity can depend upon another entity in various ways. One of the central forms of dependence is *ontological dependence*. To appreciate this form of dependence, consider the following examples: smiles ontologically depend upon mouths, events ontologically depend upon their participants, non-empty sets upon their members, tropes upon their bearers, wholes upon their parts, organisms upon their biological origins, boundaries upon the corresponding extended objects, and holes upon their hosts.[6] This notion is closely connected to other core notions in philosophical discourse such as fundamentality, substancehood, and grounding. Questions of ontological dependence are central to all areas of philosophy: in the philosophy of mind, researchers investigate how the mind ontologically depends upon the brain. In meta-ethics, one argues about the nature of the ontological dependence between evaluative and descriptive properties. In the philosophy of religion, one investigates how the world ontologically depends upon a divine being.

There are different ways to cash out ontological dependence. Some accounts focus on *existence* and say that a being depends ontologically upon another being if its *existence* depends upon the *existence* of the latter. Other accounts focus on *identity* and say that a being ontologically depends upon another being if its *identity* depends upon this other being. Whereas philosophers of the first group bring in modal notions, such as necessity and possibility, to characterise ontological dependence, philosophers of the latter group introduce the notion of *essence* (Fine, 1995: 269–70; Correia, 2008: 1014).

It is important to distinguish between causal and ontological dependence. For instance, an event (such as the breaking of a window) can causally depend upon another event (Paul's throwing a ball). But one can also ask what the breaking of the window consists in (the destruction of some molecular structures) and what needs to be there for it to take place (for instance, a window). Or one can distinguish the cause of Judy's happiness (her mother giving her a compliment)

---

[4] For this overview, see Schaffer (2009: 347–256).

[5] It it precisely this Aristotelian approach to metaphysics that has become popular again. See Schaffer (2009: 347) on this renaissance.

[6] The list can be extended. See Koslicki (2013: 1), Koslicki (2012: 188–9), and Correia (2008: 1013).

from the question of what Judy's happiness consists in (perhaps some neurons firing) and from what is required for the existence of Judy's happiness (for instance, Judy). The key point is that there can be an existential dependence relation or identity dependence between two things without there also being a causal relation, and vice versa.

In contrast with many flat-ontologists of his time (such as many Presocratics) and in agreement with Plato, Aristotle thinks that reality has an ordered structure. Consequently, when doing metaphysics, Aristotle is interested in what exists, in how to classify entities, and in the dependencies among the different categories. He is interested in the question of what things exist and he criticises his predecessors' and contemporaries' theories of what exists. (Famously, he argues with the Platonists over the question of whether Forms exist.) But Aristotle goes beyond giving a mere list of existents. He also believes that they belong to different ontological kinds and aims to produce a systematic classification of these. For instance, in the *Categories* Aristotle introduces a fourfold division of ontological classes: (1) primary substances (property-bearing individuals; e.g. Socrates); (2) secondary substances (e.g. the universal human being); (3) accidental particulars (e.g. the individual red); (4) accidental universals (e.g. the universal red). Then, in the *Metaphysics*, he further pursues this systematisation and introduces various classifications within the realm of substances by distinguishing, for instance, between perishable and non-perishable substances.

Finally, Aristotle is interested not only in classifying entities but also in determining ontological dependencies among these entities. In some cases, the dependencies are symmetrical. He calls such a symmetrical dependence 'simultaneity in nature'. In other cases, the dependencies are asymmetrical. He calls such an asymmetrical dependence 'priority in nature'. Importantly, he identifies this final task – namely to establish dependencies and to identify the fundamental items of reality – as the core subject of metaphysics. In the *Metaphysics*, Aristotle explicitly says that he is seeking the most fundamental beings in this hierarchy, the first principles (*archai*; *Metaph.* IV 1, 1003a22–1003a32; XII 1, 1069a29ff). He does not make any such programmatic statements in the *Categories*, but his investigation into the nature of substancehood and priority in the *Categories* suggests that he might have been guided by similar interests in the nature of fundamental beings. Understanding his account of ontological dependencies elucidates his view on the hierarchy of reality. For this reason, an analysis of the notions of priority and simultaneity in nature is crucial for understanding Aristotle's metaphysical system in both the *Categories* and the *Metaphysics*.

The main objective of this Element is to reconstruct Aristotle's view on the nature of ontological priority in the *Categories*.[7] I integrate Aristotle's discussions of simultaneity in nature into an analysis of ontological priority in order to arrive at a more precise account of priority in nature.[8] I intend to show that the discussions of ontological priority and ontological simultaneity illuminate one another.

Aristotle discusses priority and simultaneity in nature in three passages in the *Categories*, in chapters 7, 12, and 13. In view of the importance of the discussions of priority and simultaneity in nature[9] for understanding Aristotle's views on the structure of reality both in the *Categories* and in the *Metaphysics*, it is striking that a discussion of the central passages, especially of *Categories* 7, has not yet been offered – Ackrill, for instance, dedicates just one page to the interpretation of all the relevant passages (*Cat.* 7, 12, and 13) taken together. Other interpreters have mainly focused on Aristotle's discussions of the primacy of primary substances in *Categories* 5, 2b1–6c.[10] This Element offers the first systematic analysis of Aristotle's account of ontological dependence in these passages and shows that a thorough investigation of these passages not only leads to a better understanding of Aristotle's ontology in the *Categories* but also provides a better understanding of his metaphysical investigations in the *Metaphysics*.[11]

An analysis of priority and simultaneity in nature yields important insights into his views about the structure of reality in the *Categories*. But it is also of particular interest for understanding the relationship between the *Categories* and the *Metaphysics*, because Aristotle discusses priority in both works. For instance, the account of ontological priority that he provides in the *Categories* is in many respects more elaborate and explicit than his discussions of this topic in the *Metaphysics*. As such, it can help us to illuminate Aristotle's often cryptic remarks about ontological priority in the *Metaphysics*. For in the *Metaphysics*

---

[7] For the sake of clarity, it is important to mention that Aristotle distinguishes and discusses various senses of priority: priority in time, priority in definition, priority in knowledge, etc. This study only concentrates on what he calls 'priority in nature', 'priority in substance', and 'priority in substance and nature'.

[8] Only John Cleary (1988: 25–32) offers a brief discussion of simultaneity in nature and its relation to priority in nature.

[9] In my view, Aristotle takes up the notion 'priority in nature' from the Platonists and later renames it 'priority in substance'. See section 1.4.

[10] Only Paula Gottlieb (1993) dedicates a more detailed investigation to a part of *Categories* 7, investigating in detail Aristotle's account of perception and its relationship to his theory of relatives.

[11] I will only discuss passages in which he explicitly speaks about ontological priority. I will not deal with passages in which he discusses separation (*chōrismos*) or the explanatory priority of substantial forms.

he is more interested in putting his accounts of ontological priority to use than in discussing them as he does in the *Categories*.

I will use modern notions and logical formulations wherever I find that they are suitable to clarify Aristotle's thought. I will connect Aristotle to recent debates where I find this connection helpful for better understanding both Aristotle and the present-day debates. In contrast to some Neo-Aristotelian studies on ontological priority, I do not argue that Aristotle has a compelling, univocal account of ontological priority (Peramatzis (2011)). This study is much more critical in this regard. I will show that Aristotle has many interesting and profound ideas about ontological priority and that this concept plays a crucial role in his metaphysical system, but the study will also demonstrate that his discussion is in some respects (at least from our present-day point of view) problematic and underdeveloped. Indeed, as it turns out, he does not even develop one unified account of ontological priority, but rather a set of different, non-reducible criteria whose exact relation remains unsatisfactorily unclear.

1.2 Aristotle's Account of Ontological Priority

At present, there is a dispute in the literature on Aristotle's account of ontological priority, in particular whether he conceives of it as asymmetric *existential* dependence or as asymmetric *essential* dependence.[12] Traditionally, Aristotle's account of ontological priority has been read existentially. On this reading, put forward by Ackrill and widely accepted (Ackrill, 1963: 83; Moravcsik, 1967: 95; Loux, 1991: 16; Fine, 1995: 270), Aristotle claims that A is prior in nature to B iff necessarily, A's existence implies B's existence, but not necessarily, B's existence implies A's existence.[13]

Taking the existential construal of ontological priority to be Aristotle's considered view, many philosophers follow Aristotle and defend accounts of ontological dependence and priority in terms of existence, often tying together an understanding of ontological dependence with the notion of substancehood. For instance, Descartes writes: 'by *substance* we can understand nothing other than a thing which exists in such a way as to depend on no other thing for its *existence*' (Descartes, 1985: 210, as cited in Fine, 1995). Or Husserl: '*A content of the species A is founded upon a content of the species B* if an A can by its essence (i.e. legally, in virtue of its specific nature) not exist unless a B also exists.'[14] In addition, philosophers who are working on this issue today

---

[12] This dispute echoes a debate in present metaphysics.

[13] I use capitals in my reconstructions. These can stand for objects, properties, states of affairs, propositions, etc.

[14] Husserl (Logical Investigation III, §21, p. 475). As cited in Fine (1995).

defend existential construals of ontological priority (often by adding further qualifications: by distinguishing, for instance, rigid dependence from generic dependence or by bringing in temporal operators).[15]

However, understanding ontological priority and dependence in terms of existence is problematic.[16] (1) On the modal-existential account, it is not possible to establish an ontological priority between an object and the singleton set of this object. For the existence of Socrates necessarily implies the existence of the singleton {Socrates}, and the existence of the singleton {Socrates} necessarily implies the existence of Socrates. Yet we naturally suppose that there is such an ontological priority, namely that the singleton set ontologically depends upon its member, but not the other way round (Fine, 1995: 271).

(2) On the modal-existential account, everything depends upon necessary existents. As Kit Fine puts it: 'A different kind of difficulty arises from the case in which the "dependee" y is a necessary existent. Consider Socrates and the number 2, for example. Given that 2 necessarily exists, it is necessarily the case that 2 exists if Socrates does. But we do not want to say, on that account, that Socrates depends upon 2, that what he is depends upon what the number 2 is; and similarly for almost any other necessary existent in place of the number 2' (Fine, 1995: 271).

(3) In addition, the modal-existential approach cannot account for ontological priorities among necessarily existing items. This is problematic, since we suppose that there are such ontological priorities.

In view of the criticisms against the modal-existential account of ontological dependence, philosophers have suggested that it might be better to conceive of ontological priority in terms of *identity* or *essence*. For instance, Fine suggests that we replace the traditional modal-existential account and capture priority in terms of real definitions and essences. Using this approach, A is ontologically prior to B iff B mentions A in its definition but A does not mention B in its definition.[17]

In light of the criticisms levelled against the modal-existential account of ontological dependence and the recent suggestions to conceive of ontological priority in essentialist terms, many Aristotle scholars argue that he does not conceive of ontological dependence and priority in modal-existential terms, but rather in essentialist or explanatory terms.[18] Their strategy is to reconsider

---

[15] See Simons (1991); Moravcsik (1965: 107); Tlumak (1983). As cited in Fine (1995).

[16] Tahko and Lowe (2009) highlight that the modal existential account is specifically problematic when it is used to capture substancehood.

[17] Fine (1995: 288–9).

[18] Note that interpreters explicitly respond to the concerns raised by Fine and others. Cf. Koslicki (2013), Peramatzis (2011), and Corkum (2016).

the understanding of '*einai*' in the statements about ontological priority and to understand '*einai*' as 'what it is' rather than as 'to exist' (as in the traditional modal-existential reading). According to the essentialist reading of priority in nature, which is very popular among Neo-Aristotelian interpreters,[19] the ontological dependence in question is an *essential dependence* (Peramatzis, 2011: 244): B is ontologically dependent on A iff 'A makes B what it is', but not conversely.[20]

As I am going to argue in this study, the essentialist reading is unfortunately unpersuasive. I am not denying that in many passages Aristotle uses an essential dependence (especially when he talks about the relation between a form-matter compound and its substantial form). Certainly essential dependence plays a central role in the discussions of the *Metaphysics*. However, I argue that Aristotle is not talking about asymmetric essential dependence when speaking about *priority in nature* and *priority in substance*.

My own reading of the passages on ontological priority in Aristotle does not fit naturally with the classification of the ontological priority readings as either existential or predicative (especially essentialist). For ontological priority is often captured by means of a conditional where '*einai*' (being) shows up both in the antecedent and in the consequent, and I argue that it can be the case that '*einai*' should be read existentially in the antecedent and predicatively in the consequent, and vice versa. In my view, the understanding of '*einai*' is dependent upon the relata. If, for instance, the prior item is a property and the later item its instance, '*einai*' should be read existentially in the antecedent and predicatively in the consequent. By contrast, if both the prior and the posterior item is an object, both occurrences of '*einai*' should be read existentially. Of course, one must bear in mind that Aristotle sees a close connection between the predicative and the existential reading, since he does not accept empty terms

---

[19] Lowe (2009) and Peramatzis (2011).

[20] In addition to those who think that Aristotle has a univocal account of ontological priority (either in terms of existence (Kirwan (1993); Witt (1994); Makin (2003)) or in terms of essence (Peramatzis (2011)), there are those who maintain that he uses two distinct accounts of ontological priority, namely a modal-existential account of ontological priority and a teleological account of ontological priority (Panayides (1999) and Beere (2009)). This question arises specifically when it comes to Aristotle's discussion of ontological priority in the *Metaphysics* and is not of central concern for the *Categories*. However, I intend to show that at least one line of interpretation – namely that Aristotle has a univocal account both in the *Categories* and in the *Metaphysics* – can be seriously called into question by this study. For on my reading, Aristotle already in the *Categories* employs two non-reducibly distinct criteria. (In a second study, currently under preparation, I argue that apart from the account he puts forward in the *Categories*, he uses in some passages a second account of priority, according to which A is prior to B if A is the aim (*telos*) of a teleological process of which B is also a part (but not the end part).)

in a science, so he might even worry less than present-day readers about the precise understanding of the account of ontological priority.

1.3 Aristotle's Use of 'Einai' (Being)

Since the notion '*einai*' (being) is crucial for understanding ontological priority in Aristotle, it will be helpful to give a brief account of Aristotle's use of this notion and its various occurrences, such as the noun '*ousia*' and participle phrases such as '*to on*'.

The Greek verb '*einai*' – like its English counterpart 'being' – has a number of different uses. Charles Kahn argues convincingly that we need to make a syntactic and a semantic distinction as regards the use of the verb 'to be' in the English language (Kahn, 1966). As regards the syntactic distinction, we need to distinguish between uses of 'being' that are absolute or complete and others that are predicative or incomplete. In the latter case, the occurrence of the term 'to be' is followed by a predicate such as 'a philosopher', 'known', or 'in the black box'.[21] Kahn argues that insofar as the syntactic distinction is concerned, we find the same division in Ancient Greek (there are uses of *einai* that are complete and others that are incomplete). However, he draws attention to the fact that when we have a complete or absolute use of '*einai*', '*einai*' is used as 'to exist', but also as 'is true', 'is the case', or 'is real' (Kahn, 1966: 250). Kahn also convincingly argues that the incomplete or predicative use of '*einai*' does not merely serve to connect subject and predicate but can also be used as durative ('being' meaning 'enduring in time') or locative ('being' meaning 'being spatially located') (Kahn, 1966: 254–62). In addition, one must single out a special use, namely the 'is' of identity, within the various predicative uses. Thus, Kahn argues, as regards the Greek verb '*einai*', issues of syntax should be treated separately from issues of semantics.

As regards the interpretation of Ancient philosophers, one might wonder whether they explicitly or at least implicitly distinguished between the various uses.

At least Aristotle, one might argue, explicitly draws the relevant distinctions. In many passages Aristotle highlights that '*being*' is said in many ways (*Metaph.* IV 2; V 7; VIII 2), and there are some passages which strongly suggest that Aristotle draws a clear-cut distinction between the syntactically complete and incomplete use of *einai*, especially *An. post.* II 1, 89b32–5, *Soph. e.* V, 167a1–2, and *Soph. e.* V, 180a36–8. In these passages, Aristotle distinguishes between 'to be something' (*einai ti*) and 'to be without qualification' (*einai*

---

[21] Whereas Kahn uses the labels 'absolute' and 'predicative', Brown (1994) uses the labels 'complete' and 'incomplete'. I will follow Brown.

haplôs), which suggests that we find the dichotomy between a syntactically complete and incomplete use of *einai* at least in Aristotle.

In a detailed study of the uses of *'einai'* in Ancient philosophical writing (especially that of the Presocratics, Plato, and Aristotle), Lesley Brown questions this view and thereby pushes Kahn's results further, arguing that even within the various syntactical uses, there is no sharp distinction between the complete and incomplete uses of *'einai'* in Aristotle's philosophical writings.[22]

On the basis of these observations, Brown convincingly suggests that, even though Aristotle explicitly distinguishes a 'being *something*' from 'being *simpliciter*', he presumably did not see a semantic distinction between the 'is *something*' from the 'is *simpliciter*', and even the syntactical distinction is not as unambiguous as might be hoped. In sum, (1) Aristotle would not license the move from being *F* to being *simplicter* only for some values of F; (2) he takes there to be a close connection between questions of existence and what-it-is questions; (3) the distinctions in which he is interested, namely the difference between accidental and essential being, and the different senses of being according to the ten categories, 'cut across the syntactic distinction between complete and incomplete, and do not correspond to the semantic distinction between "exists" and the copula' (Brown, 1994: 236).

My own findings in this Element with regard to Aristotle's account of ontological priority further support Brown's and Kahn's results. Most importantly, I argue that it is often difficult to decide between an existential and a predicative reading, and that in some cases deciding between them actually makes no difference. Once again, Aristotle does not seem to present his treatment of *'einai'* as clearly as one might expect.

1.4 Aristotle, Plato, and the Academy on Ontological Priority

Since I believe that Aristotle takes up some of the criteria for ontological priority from his teacher Plato, it will be helpful to briefly look at the similarities and differences between Plato's and Aristotle's treatment of ontological priority. I have three reasons for holding the view that Aristotle inherits many of the core features of his own account of ontological priority from Plato and other Academic philosophers: (1) Aristotle himself ascribes the account of ontological priority that he himself employs to Plato in *Metaphysics* V 11; (2) in a passage from the *Eudemian Ethics* I (*EE* I 8, 1217b2–15), Aristotle again ascribes this account to Plato; and (3) we know from fragments of Xenocrates

---

[22] Brown (1994). The same is true for Plato (Brown, 1994: 216–33). See also Ackrill (1957) and Vlastos (1981) on Plato.

(another of Plato's students) that this kind of understanding of ontological priority was common in the Academy. An analysis of these passages shows that the discussion of ontological priority is an integral part of Aristotle's intellectual engagement with and criticism of Plato and other Academic philosophers, such as Xenocrates.

1.4.1 Metaphysics V 11 and Eudemian Ethics I 8

What initially supports my reading is the fact that Aristotle himself openly acknowledges this inheritance. In *Metaphysics* V 11 he explicitly ascribes an account of ontological priority in terms of an asymmetric ontological dependence to Plato:

> Some things are called prior and posterior in this way, while others are called so in nature and substance, those which can be without other things, but not the latter without them; this division was used by Plato. (*Metaph.* V 11, 1019a4–14; transl. Ross, 1924 with mod.)

A discussion of ontological priority in the *Eudemian Ethics* and a fragment by Xenocrates confirm that Aristotle ascribes this understanding of ontological priority in terms of asymmetric ontological dependence to Plato. As we are going to see, the *Eudemian Ethics* passage not only helps us to understand better how (Aristotle's) Plato thinks about the account but also how he applied it. Xenocrates' fragment shows that the account of ontological priority in terms of an asymmetric ontological dependence is widespread in the Academy.

In the *Eudemian Ethics* I 8, Aristotle discusses Plato's view of the priority in nature of the form of the Good over all other good things.[23]

Aristotle says as follows:

> [...] and it [sc. the form of the Good] is first among goods; for, if the object in which things share were destroyed, with it would go the things that share in the Form, and are called what they are called through sharing in it; and that is the way that the first stands in relation to the posterior. (*EE* I 8, 1217b2–15; transl. Woods, 1982 with mod.)

In his analysis of this passage, Peramatzis (2011: 212–16) correctly highlights that the striking notion in this characterisation is the '*anhaireisthai*'. This notion often means 'going out of existence' (or 'being taken away' or 'annihilated' or

---

23 Here and in what follows, I discuss passages in which Aristotle most plausibly discusses Plato's own view, although Aristotle does not say so explicitly, but rather speaks loosely of 'they'. See Woods (1982: 66–7). Note that Aristotle very often, when referring to Plato, speaks of 'they' rather than calling Plato by name.

'destroyed'). A textual search on the Thesaurus Linguae Graecae (*TLG*) shows that the notion is very often used to express the death of a person.[24] The point of the *TLG* search is to show that '*anhaireisthai*' is used in order to denote the transition of an object from *existence* to *non-existence*. Thus Peramatzis is correct in claiming that in view of the striking use of the term and its meaning, one has good reasons to believe that Aristotle understands Plato's conception of priority in nature as a non-reciprocal necessary existential dependence.[25]

However, some qualifications are needed here. When Aristotle says that, according to the Platonists, 'if the object in which things share were destroyed, with it would go the things that share in the Form', should we, for instance, understand this claim as saying that if the form of the good ceases to exist, its participants cease to exist *simpliciter*, or do they cease to exist *as* being good? We have seen in the previous section on Aristotle's use of '*einai*' that there are different uses of '*einai*', and I take it that there is a similar variety in the case of '*anhaireisthai*'. I propose these three conceivable ways of reading the conditional:

Existential Reading We have an existential reading of '*einai*' in both the antecedent and the consequent.
    If the form of the Good did not exist, then all the other good things (that are good) would not exist, but not the other way round.

Predicative Reading We have a predicative reading of '*einai*' in both the antecedent and the consequent.
    If the form of the Good were not good, it would not be the case that there is an x such that x is good, but not the other way round.

Mixed Reading We have an existential reading of '*einai*' in the antecedent and a predicative reading in the consequent.
    If the form of the Good did not exist, it would not be the case that there is an x such that x is good, but not the other way round (= if it were not the case that there is an x such that x is good, it is not the case that the form of the good does not exist).

In what follows, I will argue for the mixed reading. First of all, I think it is helpful to treat the best reading of '*einai*' in the antecedent and in the consequent independently.

---

[24] See for example *Pol.* V 10 1311a22; V 11, 1313a41; *Rh.* I 15, 1376a6; 1395a17.

[25] The necessity is not mentioned explicitly, but I take it to be implicitly understood. In support of this reading, note that Aristotle ascribes to Plato a modal-existential understanding of ontological priority in *Metaph.* V 11, 1019a4.

Reading of the Antecedent: Since we are talking about Platonic forms, the existential reading of the antecedent is arguably preferable over the predicative reading. For the forms are, so Plato tells us, nothing but themselves. The form of the Good is nothing but goodness. The form of Largeness is nothing but largeness. So the predicative reading of the antecedent seems forced ('if the form of the Good were not good . . .'), since the form of the Good is nothing but good. The existential reading is thus preferable: 'If the form of the Good did not exist . . .'

Reading of the Consequent: What initially speaks for the existential reading of the consequent (. . . then the good things (that are now good) would not exist) is that he says that 'with it would go the things that share in the Form'. For, according to Plato, the things that share in the forms are the substrata that receive the properties. What further supports this reading is that arguably Plato's remarks about the priority of the form of the Good in the *Republic* also imply that without the Good, nothing else would exist (Pl. *Resp.* 509b6–10). On this reading, Aristotle would be then, at least in this regard, a faithful and charitable interpreter of Plato.

However, the predicative reading of the consequent seems less problematic, for on the predicative reading, Aristotle merely states that, according to Plato, the form of the good is ontologically prior to its participants, since without there being the form of the good, the things lose their being good, but they do not cease to exist altogether.

What supports the predicative reading of the consequent is that when we analyse this passage, it seems that Aristotle is not explaining the specific priority of the form of the Good. In other words, the ontological priority of the form of the Good over its participants is just one example of a case of ontological priority among many. It looks as if he is explaining ontological priority in general and how this subsequently works out for particular cases. This suggests that the account of priority needs to be easily applicable to lots of other forms. For instance, the same account of ontological priority should also be able to be used (in the Platonic framework) in the case of the ontological priority of the form of Largeness over its participants or the form of Longness over its participants. In such cases, it is not plausible that if the form of Largeness ceases to exist *simpliciter*, the large things cease to exist *simpliciter* as well.

Since we should arguably prefer the existential reading in the protasis and the predicative reading in the apodosis, I propose that Aristotle mixes up the existential and the predicative readings: in the antecedent '*einai*' should be understood existentially, and in the consequent '*einai*' should be understood predicatively. So my reading of *EE* I 8, 1217b2–15 does not naturally fit in with the classification of the priority readings as exclusively either existential or predicative. We will find the same result when it comes to Aristotle's own discussion of ontological priority in the *Categories*.

1.4.2 Ontological Priority among Genus and Species: A Controversy between Aristotle and Xenocrates

In a fragment from Alexander of Aphrodisias, which survived only in Arabic, we learn that Xenocrates, a further pupil of Plato's in the Academy, is interested in ontological priority among species and genera. The passage reads as follows:

> Alexander says: Xenocrates says: If the relation between a species and a genus is like the relation between a part and a whole, and if a part is anterior and prior to the whole in virtue of a natural priority (for if a part is destroyed, the whole is destroyed – this in view of the fact that no whole will remain if one of its parts is lacking), whereas a part will not necessarily be destroyed if the whole to which it belongs is dissolved, since it is possible for certain parts of a whole to be eliminated while others remain), a species is likewise undoubtedly prior to its genus. (Xenocr. *Fr.* 121 Isnardi Parente; transl. Pines, 1961 with mod.)[26]

Xenocrates now applies this criterion for ontological priority to genus and species, and to parts and wholes. More precisely, he argues that because the relation between the species and the genus is a parthood relation (the species is a part of the genus), and because a part is ontologically prior[27] to a whole, the species is ontologically prior to the genus.

This surviving text strongly suggests, together with the passage from the *Eudemian Ethics*, that many philosophers in the Academy were interested in understanding both the nature of ontological priority and its extension. In the passage in question (Xenocr. *Fr.* 121 IP), Xenocrates conceives of ontological priority in terms of asymmetric existential dependence.

Xenocrates' argument and claims are interesting for several reasons. First, it shows that there evidently was a discussion and disagreement within the Academy (and philosophers close to the Academy such as Aristotle) as to whether the genus is ontologically prior to the species. Coming from Plato, one would evidently take the Academic doctrine to be that the genus is prior to the species. Surprisingly, Aristotle himself argues in the *Categories* that the genus is prior in substance to the species.[28] Now we see that there is an Academic

---

[26] See the discussion of this fragment in Pines (1961) and Rashed (2004).

[27] Aristotle speaks here of 'priority in nature', which I assume to be ontological priority. See more on Aristotle's use of 'priority in nature' in the concluding remarks of this Element.

[28] It is not easy to accommodate Aristotle's claim that the genus is ontologically prior to the species precisely because in relevant respects he moved away from the Academic dogma by assigning to ordinary particular objects the status of primacy substances.

philosopher, namely Xenocrates, who questions this dogma. For, according to him, the species is ontologically more fundamental than the genus.[29]

Second, it shows that within the Academic tradition there are cases where ontological priority is conceived of in purely existential terms. When analysing the *Eudemian Ethics* passage, we have seen that we should understand '*anhaireisthai*' in the antecedent in existential terms. Here, in Xenocrates' fragment, we should understand '*anhaireisthai*' *both* in the antecedent *and* in the consequent existentially. It seems to me to be important to take the relata into account when we decide whether we should prefer an existential reading of '*anhaireisthai*' or a predicative reading. Given that the forms are the causes of the properties of objects, a predicative reading of '*anhaireisthai*' and '*einai*' is much more attractive than in a case where the relata are objects (in Xenocrates' case, parts and wholes).

1.4.3 Divisiones Aristotelis

Finally, in the *Divisiones Aristotelis* 64, a collection of short texts about the relationship between terms (Mutschmann, 1907), ontological priority is again captured in terms of asymmetric ontological dependence, which is here best understood as asymmetric existential dependence:

> 'Prior' is said in five ways: For it is said in nature, in time, in capacity, in setting, in order. [â€¦] Something is prior in nature, for example, the one is prior to the two, and the part to the whole, and the genus to the species, and in general everything that does not reciprocally destroy each other. In these cases, that which destroys the other thing with itself is prior in nature, and that which is destroyed is posterior in nature. For example, if the number one is destroyed, the two is destroyed and every number, but if the two is destroyed nothing prevents there being the number one. Therefore, the number one is prior in nature to the number two. Likewise if the part is destroyed the whole is destroyed, but if the whole does not exist, nothing prevents the existence of the part. (*Divisiones Aristotelis*, Mutschmann, 1907: 64)

Its authorship is contested, but scholars agree that the author must have been a member of Aristotle's school. The fragment on priority is interesting because

---

[29] Aristotle is still concerned with this issue in the *Metaphysics* and he treats it there as an ongoing debate. It is interesting to see that Xenocrates is part of the debate and an interlocutor for Aristotle. See Aristotle's discussions in *Metaphysics* III: 'Again, whether the principles and *Element*s of things are the classes, or the parts present in each thing into which it is divided; and if they are the classes, whether they are the classes that are predicated proximately of the individuals, or the highest classes, e.g. whether animal or man is the first principle and the more independent of the individual instance?' (*Metaph*. III 1, 995b27–31; transl. Ross, 1924). Cf. *Metaph*. III 3, 998a20–999a2.

it confirms my central claims: (1) that there are major discussions in the Academy and in Aristotle's school about how to conceive of the concept and extension of ontological priority; and (2) that within the Academic tradition there are cases where ontological priority is conceived of in purely existential terms.

In this passage Pseudo-Aristotle first draws distinctions between different kinds of priority (as does Aristotle frequently in the passages where he theorises about priority (cf. *Cat.* 12; *Metaph.* V 11 and IX 8)). When discussing priority in nature (*proteron tēi phusei*), Pseudo-Aristotle gives an account of it and its extension. The account he provides, though slightly differing in its formulation, is the same as the one we find in Aristotle's discussion in the *Eudemian Ethics*, in the Xenocrates fragment, and, as we will see in the following sections, in the *Categories* (*Cat.* 7, 7b22–8a12).

1.4.4 The Academy and Aristotle

An analysis of the passages under discussion strongly suggests that both Aristotle and Academic philosophers understand ontological priority as an asymmetric dependence in being. I have argued that the terms '*einai*' and '*anhaireisthai*' in the statements about ontological priority can be understood both predicatively (excluding the essentialist reading) and existentially. Sometimes Aristotle (and the Academics) use different understandings of '*einai*' and '*anhaireisthai*' within the same statement about priority. This is the case, for instance, in *EE* I 8, 1217b2–15.

On the basis of our texts, it seems that the Academics use only asymmetric dependence in being as a criterion for ontological priority. This suggests that asymmetric dependence in being is a necessary and sufficient condition for priority for Academic philosophers. In the following chapters, I argue that Aristotle adds a further condition to the account of ontological priority, so that asymmetric dependence in being is no longer a necessary condition for ontological priority, although it remains a sufficient condition. In addition, we will discover that while Plato and other Academics might not yet have used modal operators in accounts of ontological dependence,[30] they nonetheless form an integral part of Aristotle's account of dependence.

On my reading, the disagreement between Academic philosophers and Aristotle on ontological priority does not derive from their different views on the precise understanding of asymmetric dependence in being, as some have

---

[30] We find the modal operator mentioned in *Metaph.* V 11, 1019a4–14 and Xenocr. *Fr.* 121 IP, but not in *EE* I 8, 1217b2–15 and *Divisiones Aristotelis* 64.

claimed (Peramatzis, 2011: 212–16); rather it is due to their different views on what satisfies the conditions of being ontologically prior.

1.5 Section Overview

The structure of this Element is as follows:[31] the second section offers a detailed account of Aristotle's understanding of priority in nature in *Categories* 12 and 13. I argue that Aristotle proposes a disjunctive account of priority in nature consisting of the following two conditions:

(1) A is ontologically prior to B if necessarily B's being implies A's being, but not necessarily, A's being implies B's being.
(2) A is ontologically prior to B if necessarily A's and B's being symmetrically imply each other, and A's being is a cause of B's being.

I argue that implication of being can be understood either existentially or predicatively. I then argue that an existential reading is preferable to a predicative reading in most cases.

The third section offers a close reading of *Categories* 7. I address some concerns concerning the treatment of dependencies among relatives. By taking into account Aristotle's discussions of simultaneity in nature, I argue that he distinguishes between different kinds of dependencies relative to what kind of entities he is discussing (for example, whether he is talking about necessarily existing or contingently existing entities, entities existing in time, or properties and objects).

The fourth section examines one of the most controversial chapters in the entire *Categories*, namely *Categories* 5, where Aristotle asserts the primacy of the primary substances. On my reading, Aristotle accounts for the primacy of the primary substances on the grounds that they are the ultimate subjects of predication.

The final section summarises the major outcomes of the previous sections and explains why Aristotle's discussion might be open to criticism. It concludes with a look at how the discussion of ontological priority in the *Categories* might be relevant for understanding Aristotle's discussion of ontological priority in the *Metaphysics*.

---

[31] Note that my order involves moving backwards through this work. I start with the chapters in which Aristotle's exposition is especially clear (chapters 12 and 13). I then move to chapter 7, which offers important refinements. I conclude with chapter 5, which contains an important discussion of the primary substances that has often been seen as an application of his account of ontological priority.

2 Ontological Priority in Aristotle's *Categories* 12 and 13

2.1 Introduction

This section offers the first systematic analysis of Aristotle's discussion of onto-logical priority in *Cat.* 12 and 13. On my reading, Aristotle puts forward two non-reducible criteria for priority in nature that are individually sufficient and disjunctively necessary and sufficient for priority in nature. According to the first criterion, A is prior in nature to B if necessarily B's being implies A's being but not necessarily A's being implies B's being. According to the sec-ond criterion, A is prior in nature to B if necessarily A's being and B's being symmetrically imply each other and A's being is in some way a cause (*aition pōs*) of B's being. I argue that in both criteria, 'being' can be understood either existentially or veridically but never essentially.[32]

2.2 Priority of the Genus over the Species in *Categories* 13

In *Cat.* 13, 15a4–7 Aristotle claims that genera are prior in nature to species. In this subsection I argue that in *Cat.* 13 Aristotle conceives of priority in nature between a genus and a species in terms of non-symmetric necessary existential dependence between the objects that fall under the genus and the species.

Aristotle says as follows (and we will see on the next page that there are also several different readings of this passage):

> Genera, however, are always prior [sc. in nature] to species since they do not reciprocate as to implication of being; e.g. if there is a fish, then there is an animal, but if there is an animal then there is not necessarily a fish. (*Cat.* 13, 15a4–7)[33]

In this passage Aristotle is concerned with the asymmetric dependence between two universals,[34] namely the universal 'animal' and the universal 'fish'.

The interpretation of the priority depends upon how one answers the follow-ing two sets of questions:

---

[32] In agreement with the essentialist reading, I argue that essential dependencies among the relata of ontological priority or simultaneity relations play an important role when it comes to deter-mining what it is to be prior to or simultaneous with another item, yet I do not identify priority in nature with asymmetric essential dependence.

[33] I justify this translation later in this section.

[34] 'Genera, however, are always prior to species'. These are, for Aristotle, universals. The view that Aristotle is concerned here with universals is supported by the fact that when Aristotle is discussing simultaneity in nature relations that regard genera and species, he ultimately aims to determine the relation between universals and not between properties or instances of universals. In *Cat.* 13, 14b33–15a4 he says that 'animal' is subdivided into 'bird' and 'beast' and 'fish'. He is, thus, clearly talking about the taxonomy of the universal 'animal' rather than its instances or the instantiation of the property being an animal'.

(1) Are the terms ('fish' (*enhudron*); 'animal' (*zōon*)) subjects or predicates in
     the conditionals?
(2) How should 'being' (*einai*) be interpreted? In particular, does Aristotle say
     something about the existence of the items in question?

I take it that among the great variety of conceivable interpretations, there are
only three viable options:

(1) A *predicative* reading, according to which the ontological priority of the
     genus 'animal' over the species 'fish' consists in a predicative priority of
     the genus over the species. On this reading, 'fish' and 'animal' are taken
     to be predicates and '*einai*' is read predicatively.

     Necessarily,[35] if something is a fish, it is an animal, but not necessarily, if
     something is an animal, it is a fish.
(2) An *existential-universal* reading, according to which the ontological prior-
     ity of the genus 'animal' over the species 'fish' consists in an existential
     priority *of the genus over the species*. On this reading, 'fish' and 'ani-
     mal' are taken to be subjects and stand for universals. '*Einai*' is read
     existentially.

     Necessarily, if the species 'fish' exists, the genus 'animal' exists, but not
     necessarily, if the genus 'animal' exists, the species 'fish' exists.
(3) An *existential-instances* reading, according to which the ontological prior-
     ity of the genus 'animal' over the species 'fish' consists in an existential
     priority *of the instances of the genus over the instances of species*. On this
     reading, 'fish' and 'animal' are taken to be subjects and stand for instances
     of universals. '*Einai*' is read existentially.

     Necessarily, if a 'fish' exists, an 'animal' exists, but not necessarily, if an
     'animal' exists, a 'fish' exists.

In the following, I discuss each of the three readings. I will contend that (3) is
the most promising option.

The Predicative Reading On the predicative reading, the ontological priority
between the universals 'fish' and 'animal' consists in a predicative dependence
between the properties 'being a fish' and 'being an animal'. On this reading, the
genus is prior in nature to the species, since necessarily if something belongs
to the species, it belongs to the genus, but not necessarily, if something belongs
to the genus, it belongs to the species.

---

[35] I assume that Aristotle implicitly uses a modal operator ('necessarily') already in the first
conditional. In fact, one could take the '*anangkē*' to govern both conditionals.

What seems to support this more sophisticated reading is a comparative analysis with similar passages in the *Analytics*. Susanne Bobzien, in analysing similar conditionals in the *Prior Analytics*, argues that we should prefer the predicative reading in the case of such conditionals. Her prevailing motivation for this reading is that if we read such conditionals predicatively, they are more easily reformulable into proper syllogisms. And we are generally operating under the assumption that such a reformulation is desirable.

For instance, in *Prior Analytics* I 32, 47a28–31 Aristotle says that:

ἀνθρώπου ὄντος ἀνάγκη ζῷον εἶναι

καὶ ζῴου οὐσίαν,

ἀνθρώπου ὄντος ἀνάγκη οὐσίαν εἶναι.

First, a literal translation that does not commit us to any reading:

being a human being necessarily *being an animal*

being an animal necessarily *being a substance*

being a human being necessarily *being a substance*

Being a human being, being a substance, and *being an animal* can be read in two ways.

Predicatively:

If it is a human being, it is necessarily an animal.

If it is an animal, it is necessarily a substance.

Hence, if it is a human being, it is necessarily a substance.

Existentially:

Necessarily, if a human being exists, an animal exists.

Necessarily, if an animal exists, a substance exists.

Hence, necessarily, if a human being exists, a substance exists.[36]

Bobzien opts for the predicative reading, since she thinks that it is possible on the predicative reading to reformulate elegantly into a syllogism. She aims

---

[36] Note that the necessity operator in the two reconstructions is placed differently. Aristotle's use of modal operators is not as precise as one might wish (sometimes he drops them altogether). For this reason I think that both reconstructions are legitimate readings of the Greek.

to show how this reformulation could be done, first of all, by tidying up the formulation. On Bobzien's reading, the grammatical form of the argument reads as follows (Bobzien, 2000: 92):

τοῦ Α ὄντος ἀνάγκη τὸ Β εἶναι

τοῦ Β ὄντος ἀνάγκη τὸ Γ εἶναι

τοῦ Α ὄντος ἀνάγκη τὸ Γ εἶναι

being A, it is necessarily B

being B, it is necessarily C

being A, it is necessarily C

Bobzien holds that this argument becomes a proper syllogism if it is reformulated in the following way (Bobzien, 2000: 93):

substance belongs to every animal

animal belongs to every human being

therefore substance belongs to every human being

Put into *modus Barbara* this reads as follows:

C belongs to every B

B belongs to every A

therefore C belongs to every A

Bobzien argues that on the assumption that Aristotle takes the argument in *Prior Analytics* I 32, 47a28–31 to be reformulable in the aforementioned manner (a valid syllogism with *modus Barbara*), we should understand the two formulations as being more or less equivalent. This suggests that we should understand the premises and conclusion as follows:

If anything is T_A, it is necessary that it is T_B.

Bobzien suggests that 'this is a natural way of paraphrasing sentences of the kind T_A ὄντος ἀνάγκη T_B εἶναι.[37] For they have exactly two terms (T_A, T_B), and there is no singular subject term explicitly mentioned in either the genitive absolute or the main clause' (Bobzien, 2000: 93).

---

[37] Cf. Arist. *Top.* 112a17–19, ἄνθρωπον εἶναι for 'something is a man'.

Since the conditionals in *An. pr.* I 32, 47a28–31 and in *Cat.* 13, 15a6–7 are quite similar, Bobzien's analysis strongly suggests that we should prefer the predicative reading of '*einai*' and take Aristotle as talking about properties in the conditional. The predicative reading reads as follows:

> Necessarily, for all *x*, S*x* → G*x*, but ¬ necessarily for all *x*, G*x* → S*x*. (S = being an instance of the species; G = being an instance of the genus.)

On this reading, the ontological priority of the genus G over the species S consists in a predicative priority of being G over being S.

Problem for the predicative reading: There is a grammatical aspect that speaks against Bobzien's reconstruction, namely that in the case in question Aristotle employs a genitive absolute. On Bobzien's reading, the three conditionals –

> If it is a human being, it is necessarily an animal.
>
> If it is an animal, it is necessarily a substance.
>
> Hence, if it is a human being, it is necessarily a substance.

– all have the same subject. But since they all have the same subject, one does not expect a genitive absolute, but a participle and predicate in the nominative, or rather in the accusative (since we are in reported speech). So, on Bobzien's reading, the Greek should rather read:

> ἀνθρωπόν ὄντα ἀνάγκη ζῷον εἶναι
>
> καὶ ζῷον οὐσίαν,
>
> ἀνθρωπόν ὄντα ἀνάγκη οὐσίαν εἶναι.

In short, I think that if Aristotle had wanted to say what Bobzien claims he says, he would have formulated it in a different way. For this reason I think that the predicative reading of *An. pr.* I 32, 47a22–31 suggested by Bobzien and an analogous predicative reading of *Cat.* 13, 15a4–7 is unsatisfactory.[38] I

---

[38] Note that even if the predicative reading is the correct reading of the passage and '*einai*' should be understood predicatively and not existentially, the reading would have an existential implication, since terms are not empty in Aristotle's syllogistic.

find an existential reading of both passages more convincing.[39] I will discuss the existential reading of *Cat.* 13, 15a4–7 in the next section.

In *Cat.* 12, 14a29–35 Aristotle also speaks of implication of being. I will discuss this passage in Section 2.3, but here I would point out that as regards the interpretation of that passage, the predicative reading is even more problematic: Aristotle says there that 'and if half is, double is' (καὶ ἡμίσεος ὄντος διπλάσιόν ἐστιν). On Bobzien's reconstruction, this would read: being A, it is (necessarily) B. Half belongs to every double. This is evidently false. In this case we should opt for an existential reading, and if we use an existential reading in this case, one might think that we should also use an existential reading in *Cat.* 13, 15a4–7 and *An. pr.* I 32, 47a22–31.

The Existential Reading   Rather than reading '*einai*' in *Cat.* 13, 15a4–7 predicatively, it is also possible to read it existentially, as meaning 'to exist'. There are two different existential readings, though. They agree insofar as both take 'fish' and 'animal' in the protasis and the apodosis to be subjects. They differ insofar as the first takes these terms to stand for universals, while the second takes the terms to stand for objects that fall under these universals. I will argue for the second view, but let us begin by examining the first reading.

On the existential-universal reading, Aristotle formulates in this passage an existential dependence between the universal 'animal' and the universal 'fish', where the universals function themselves in the conditional. It reads as follows:

> Necessarily, if the universal 'fish' exists, the universal 'animal' exists, but not necessarily, if the universal 'animal' exists, the universal 'fish' exists.

This reading is straightforward. The genus is prior to the species, since the existence of the *species* depends upon the existence of the *genus* but not the other way around.

However, the reading has some major problems.

(1) The first concern is a grammatical one. Aristotle does not use an article before 'fish' and 'animal' in *Cat.* 13, 15a4–7. This suggests that he is not talking

---

[39] There is, of course, a close connection between the existential reading, which I will defend – i.e. that we should understand the conditionals rather as follows: 'Necessarily, $\exists x\ Sx \rightarrow \exists y\ Gy$' – and the predicative reading for which Bobzien is arguing – i.e. 'Necessarily, for all $x\ Sx \rightarrow Gx$'; namely that since animal is predicated of all human beings, the existence of a human being implies the existence of an animal. The predication explains why an existential dependence holds, but the predication is not itself the object of the conditionals that Aristotle formulates here.

about determinate entities but indeterminate ones. It is some fish or other and not the determinate species 'fish'. Note that Aristotle uses the article earlier in the same section when he discusses the genus and the species (14b35–6: *to pnēton, tōi pezōi kai tōi enhudrōi*; 14b37–15a1: *to zōion, to ptēnon, to pezon, to enhudron*; 15a2–3: *to pezon, to ptēnon, to enhudron*). If he were to continue to speak about the universals themselves in *Cat.* 13, 15a4–7, he would probably continue to use an article.

(2) The second concern is a metaphysical one. Aristotle claims that 'not necessarily if animal exists, fish exists', yet, at the same time, he believes that the species 'fish' necessarily exists. According to a simple reading of the existential account, the claim is simply false, given that he thinks that the species 'fish' necessarily exists.[40] The question is whether Aristotle is making a blatant error here.

In light of the difficulties of this *existential-universal* reading, I think that the second existential reading – which takes 'fish' and 'animal' to be objects that fall under the universals rather than as the universals themselves – to be more promising. On this reading, the ontological priority among the genus 'animal' and the species 'fish' consists in an existential priority *of the instances of the genus over the instances of the species*:

> Necessarily, if a fish exists, an animal exists, but not necessarily, if an animal exists, a fish exists.

The existential-instances reading has the advantage over the existential-universal reading in that it can account for the fact that Aristotle does not use the article in the conditional (since it takes Aristotle to be speaking about some fish or other and some animal or other).

However, this reading shares with the existential-universal reading the difficulty that it is false that 'not necessarily, if an animal exists, a fish exists'. This is because Aristotle believes that species are by necessity instantiated, which means that, by necessity, there always exists something that is a fish.

Nevertheless, despite this significant difficulty, since it has fewer problems than the existential-universal reading but shares that reading's virtues in comparison with the predicative reading, I take it to be most promising interpretation overall.

---

[40] Note that the essentialists are committed to reading this conditional as false as well, since as their reading would have it: 'If fish is what it is, animal is what it is, but if animal is what it is, fish is not necessarily what it is.' The species 'fish' is necessarily what it is, according to Aristotle.

The Essentialist Reading Some interpreters have argued that Aristotle uses an 'essentialist' account of ontological priority in both the *Categories* and the *Metaphysics*, according to which A is prior in nature to B if A makes B what it is but B does not make A what it is.[41] This passage strongly speaks against the reading that Aristotle conceives of ontological priority in terms of asymmetric *essential* dependence. On the face of it, the essentialist reading of priority in nature makes sense. Aristotle says that the genus is prior in nature to the species (*Cat.* 13, 15a4–7) and the genus is essentially prior to the species. However, the essential dependence does not capture the priority in nature as Aristotle develops it here. When he explains the priority of the genus over the species, he does not say that the genus is prior to the species because the genus makes the species what it is. Rather he speaks of asymmetric 'implication of being'. On the essentialist reading (reading '*einai*' as 'being what it is' in the conditional), the passage reads as follows:

> Necessarily, if fish is what it is, then animal is what it is, but, not necessarily, if animal is what it is, fish is what it is.

On the essentialist reading, the essence of fish determines the essence of animal. This is arguably not what Aristotle wants to claim in this passage and elsewhere. The essentialist overtranslation of *einai* leads to this problem.

In agreement with the essentialist reading, I argue that essential dependencies among the relata of ontological priority play an important role when it comes to determining what it is to be prior to another item, since it often explains why an existential dependence holds. For instance, in this case the fact that the genus is part of the essence of the species explains why it is necessarily the case that if a fish exists, an animal exists. Yet one should not identify priority in nature with asymmetric essential dependence.

2.3 Priority of the Number One over the Number Two in *Categories* 12

In this subsection I argue that also in *Cat.* 12 Aristotle conceives of priority in nature in terms of asymmetric necessary implication of existence.

In *Cat.* 12 Aristotle introduces five different kinds of priority: (1) priority in time; (2) asymmetric implication of being; (3) priority in order; (4) priority in value;[42] and (5) symmetric implication of being with an explanatory priority

---

[41] Lowe (2009); Corkum (2008); Koslicki (2013); Peramatzis (2011).

[42] He also calls this kind of priority 'priority in nature'. I do not discuss this kind of priority in nature, since it is clearly not connected with ontological dependence.

of the one item over the other.[43] In this subsection, I discuss (2) (= asymmetric implication of being), in particular how to understand the priority relation and where it applies. I discuss (5) in the next subsection of this section. (1), (3), and (4) are not germane to my question.

Aristotle says (and we will see below that, as in the case of the priority between genus and species, there are also several different readings of this passage – the interpretative difficulties are exactly the same):

> Second, [prior is] what *does not reciprocate as to implication of being*. For example, one is prior to two because if there are two it follows at once that there is one, whereas if there is one, there are not necessarily two, so that the implication of the other's being does not hold reciprocally from one; and that from which the implication of being does not hold reciprocally is thought to be prior. (*Cat.* 12, 14a29–35; transl. Ackrill, 1963 with mod.)[44]

In this passage Aristotle aims to establish an ontological priority among two numbers, namely the number one and the number two. He claims that there is an asymmetric implication of being between the number 'one' and the number 'two'.

Note that he also uses the expression 'implication of being' (κατὰ τὴν τοῦ εἶναι ἀκολούθησιν) in *Cat.* 13 when he discusses the ontological dependence between genus and species, and, as in the discussion in *Cat.* 13, he uses conditionals in order to grasp the priority.

One might think that, as in the genus and species case, there are three ways of interpreting this passage: (1) a predicative reading;[45] (2) an existential reading whereby the terms are universals;[46] and (3) an existential reading whereby the terms are objects that fall under the universals.[47]

I will now show that neither (1) nor (2) is a satisfactory reading. The problems in this case are the same as those facing the predicative and the

---

[43] There is the following peculiarity of the discussion. At the beginning of the section, Aristotle announces that he is presenting four notions of priority. After having discussed four types of priority, he says that there is an additional kind of priority. This has led to discussions of whether or not this additional paragraph was part of the original draft of the section. A reason to believe that it was part of the original draft is that he refers to this kind of priority in section 13 in his discussion of simultaneity in nature (*Cat.* 14b28–9).

[44] I justify this translation later in this section.

[45] Necessarily, if something is two, it is one, but not necessarily, if something is one, it is two. (I assume that Aristotle implicitly uses a modal operator ('necessarily') already in the first conditional. In fact, one could take the '*anangkē*' to govern both conditionals.)

[46] Necessarily, if the universal 'two' exists, the universal 'one' exists, but not necessarily, if the universal 'one' exists, the universal 'two' exists.

[47] Necessarily, if a 'two' exists, a 'one' exists, but not necessarily, if a 'one' exists, a 'two' exists.

existential-universal reading in the earlier passage. As in the previous discussion on the priority of genus and species, I think that (3) is the most promising option.

Let us first turn our attention to the predicative reading. On the predicative reading, the number one is prior to the number two, since the predication of 'being two' implies the predication of 'being one' but the predication of 'being one' does not imply the predication of 'being two'.

On the predicative reading, both properties are predicated of the same object.[48] Clearly, Aristotle cannot mean that in this case both the properties are predicated of the same object. For when two is predicted of an object, one is not predicated of it (one could only be predicated of a part of it). Hence the predicative reading is unconvincing.

The existential-universal reading of this passage runs into the same problem as the existential-universal reading of the priority among genus and species. (a) There is a grammatical problem: Aristotle does not use articles in the antecedent and the consequent. This suggests that he is not speaking of determinate numbers. Note that he does use articles in the priority clause. He says: 'The one is prior to the two' (*Cat.* 12a31). (b) Given that both the universal number 'one' and the universal number 'two' necessarily exist, neither can exist without the other, so we cannot account for the priority simply in terms of a modal-existential account. For on this reading, Aristotle's claim that 'if there exists one there do not necessarily exist two' is simply false, because the number two necessarily exists. And his claim that 'if there exist two it follows at once that there exists one' seems trivial, because whatever you use as the antecedent, the conditional will be true. As noted earlier, so long as we cannot ascribe to Aristotle a more sophisticated account of implication, this reading remains unsatisfactory.

Since both the predicative and the existential-universal reading run into grammatical and metaphysical problems, I think that (as in the case of the genus and species) the existential-instances reading is the more promising one. Although it does not avoid the metaphysical problem (since Aristotle believes that instances of the number one and the number two necessarily exist), it at least avoids the grammatical problem. I take it that we understand the priority best as follows:

> Necessarily, if a 'two' exists, a 'one' exists, but not necessarily, if a 'one' exists, a 'two' exists.

---

[48] Cf. *Cat.* 13, 15a4–7: both 'being a fish' and 'being an animal' are predicated of the same object.

Necessarily, $\exists x\, Tx \rightarrow \exists y\, Oy$, but $\neg$ necessarily, $\exists x\, Ox \rightarrow \exists y\, Ty$. (O = being one; T = being two.)[49]

2.4 Priority in Nature and Truth-Making

I now argue that Aristotle proposes a second criterion for priority in nature that is non-reducible to the previous criterion for priority (as just discussed). Aristotle develops this second account in *Cat.* 12, 14b9–23.

The passage is not only of interest because Aristotle offers a second account of priority in nature; it is also pertinent because his discussion clarifies some aspects of his notion of the 'implication of being'. For so far we have seen that 'being' in 'implication of being' should be understood existentially.

In *Cat.* 12, 14b9–23, I argue, Aristotle uses 'being' in 'implication of being' in two ways, namely existentially and veridically. In this passage he says:

> There are, then, this many ways of speaking of the prior. There would seem, however, to be another manner of priority besides those mentioned. For of things which reciprocate as to implication of *being*, that which is in some way the cause of the other's being might reasonably be called prior by nature. And that there are some such cases is clear. For man *is* reciprocates as to implication of *being* with the true sentence about it: if man *is*, the sentence whereby we say that man *is* is true, and reciprocally – since if the sentence whereby we say that man *is* is true, man is. But whereas the true sentence is in no way the cause of the object's *being*, the actual thing does seem in some way the cause of the statement's being true: For it is because the object is or is not that a sentence is called true or false. Thus there are five ways in which one thing might be called prior to another. (*Cat.* 12, 14b9–23, my italics.)

The criterion for priority that Aristotle puts forward in this passage can be formalised as follows:

> A is prior in nature to B if (1) A's and B's being symmetrically implies each other and (2) A's being is in some way the cause of B's being.

---

[49] If I am right and Aristotle does implicitly use temporal operators in the accounts of dependence whenever he speaks about items existing in time, then the dependence should be conceived of as non-symmetric necessary *synchronic* existential dependence. This account can be formulated as follows:

One is prior in nature to two since $\Box \forall t((\text{at t: } \exists x\, Tx) \rightarrow (\text{at } t\text{: } \exists y\, Oy))$ and $\neg\Box\forall t((\text{at t: } \exists x\, Ox) \rightarrow (\text{at } t\text{: } \exists y\, Ty))$.

Whereas something that is a two cannot exist at a time unless something that is a one exists at that time, something that is a one can exist at a time without something that is a two existing at that time.

Aristotle says in this passage that in the case of a symmetric ontological dependence, there might still hold a priority relation between the two relata, namely if one item is the cause (*to aition hopôsoun* or simply *aition*) of the being of the other item. The relata of the priority are objects and sentences about those objects.[50]

He illustrates this claim by using the species 'man' and the sentence 'man is'. He claims that these two convert (= reciprocate) as to implication of being.[51] How should we understand this? Most importantly, how should we understand the important occurrences of '*einai*' (being) in this passage (italicised in the text above)?

I argue that when Aristotle speaks here about mutual implication of being, he wants to say that *the existence* of a man implies *the being true* of the sentence 'man exists' and the *being true* of the sentence 'man exists' implies the existence of a man. I call this a *hybrid* reading, since on this reading Aristotle uses two different understandings of '*einai*' when he speaks about a mutual 'implication of being'. This is a new reading of this passage. It differs from two earlier interpretations in that it does not understand '*einai*' univocally, as meaning either 'to exist' or 'to be true' in all relevant cases.

In the following I discuss these two previous interpretations and argue that neither is fully satisfactory:

(1) *An existential reading*: Ackrill suggests that we should understand the relevant occurrences of '*einai*' existentially. On this reading, the mutual implication of being reads as follows:

> The existence of the true sentence 'man is' implies the existence of the state of affairs 'man is' and the existence of the state of affairs 'man is' implies the existence of the true sentence 'man is'.

The problem with this reading is that it does not adequately capture the way in which Aristotle explains the priority in the example.[52] Aristotle does not say that the existence of man implies the existence of the true proposition and conversely. He says that the existence of man implies the *being true* of the

---

[50] Note that 'object' at 14b19–21 denotes just those items that are relevant for the truth value of sentences about them. This reading has also been suggested by Crivelli (2004: 104): 'The occurrences of "object" at 14b19–21 denote those (composite or non-composite) objects that are crucial to the truth or falsehood of assertions concerning them; [...].'

[51] I agree with Crivelli that the occurrence of 'it' (*peri autou*) in 'the true sentence about it' (14b15) refers to the species 'man'.

[52] Ackrill (1963: 111–12) himself already expresses some concern over his own reading: 'It is odd to call this a reciprocal implication of existence: we should not say that the existence of there being a man implies and is implied by the existence of the true statement that there is a man, nor does Aristotle adhere to this way of speaking in his discussion of the example.'

proposition 'man exists' ('if man *is*, the sentence whereby we say that man *is* is true, and reciprocally – since if the sentence whereby we say that man *is* is true, man is; [...] the actual thing does seem in some way the cause of the statement's being true: For it is because the object is or is not that a sentence is called true or false').

(2) *A veridical reading*: On this reading, we should read the crucial occurrences of '*einai*' rather as 'being true' in the sense outlined in *Metaphysics* IX. This reading has been suggested by Crivelli.[53] On this reading, 'man' is true converts into the sentence 'man is' being true ('the species man "is" in the sense of being true, i.e. exists, when and only when the assertion "Man is" is true'[54]). As we have seen, according to Aristotle, for a non-composite item, 'to be' in the sense of being true is simply to exist.[55] (I assume that for Aristotle the universal man is a non-composite item; Crivelli, 2004: 104.)

On the veridical reading, Aristotle claims that it is not the sentence 'man is' being true that makes 'man' being true, but the other way around: since man is true, the sentence 'man is' is true. On this reading, an existential implication follows from the veridical reading (since a non-composite item's being true is nothing but its existence), but we do not read the '*einai*' in implication of being immediately as meaning 'to exist'.

Crivelli tries to correct the deficiency of the purely existential reading (its lack of sensitivity to the connection between truth and being) insofar as he now argues that all relevant occurrences of '*einai*' should be understood veridically. An advantage of his reading is that '*einai*' in 'implication of being' is understood univocally. A further advantage is that Crivelli can provide a more sophisticated account of the connection between the existential and the veridical reading of '*einai*' in this passage.

Although Crivelli's reading is supported by a sophisticated theory of truth in Aristotle, I do not find his reading entirely convincing. I think that the biggest

---

[53] Crivelli (2004: 104): 'the crucial occurrences of "to be" should be understood as expressing the "being" in the sense of being true discussed in *Metaphysics* Θ; [...].'

[54] Crivelli (2004: 104). Crivelli (2004: 103) claims that Aristotle makes precisely this point in 1051b33–1052a1: 'With "being" as truth and "not being" as falsehood, one [a composite item] is true if it is composed, while it is false if it is not composed, the other [a non-composite item] is [exists] if it is a "being" in this sense [if it "is" in the sense of being true], while if it "is not" in this sense [if it "is not" in the sense of being false] it is not [does not exist].' Crivelli now cites 14b11–22 (where Aristotle discusses priority in nature) as an example of an existential assertion concerning a non-composite item. This is just the passage where Aristotle puts forward the second criterion for priority in nature.

[55] A case of an existential assertion concerning a composite item can be found in *Metaphysics* IX 10, 1051b6–8: 'It is not because we think truly that you are pale, that you are truly pale; it is because you are truly pale that we who say this are speaking truly.' Cf. *Int.* 18a39–b3; 19a33–5.

problem for Crivelli's reading is that Aristotle uses '*alēthēs*' as a predicate in 14b16, 14b17, and 14b20. Why would he do so if '*einai*' ought to be understood veridically in this passage? On Crivelli's reading, Aristotle would have been more straightforward if he had just dropped '*alēthēs*' as a predicate. As it stands, Crivelli must explain why Aristotle highlights the fact that he speaks about truth in the case of a sentence but that he does not do so when he speaks about the object.

Since I find neither the existential nor the veridical reading entirely convincing for the reasons given, I suggest that one should embrace a hybrid reading. On the hybrid reading, *the existence* of a man implies *the being true* of the sentence 'man exists', and the *being true* of the sentence 'man exists' implies the existence of a man. When Aristotle speaks about 'mutual implication of being' in this case, he understands 'being' as being open between the meaning 'to exist' and 'to be true'.

The advantage of this reading is that it captures most adequately Aristotle's discussion. The disadvantage is that 'being' in 'mutual implication of being' is no longer understood univocally.[56]

As already stated, the second criterion can be formalised as follows:

> A is prior in nature to B if (1) A's and B's being symmetrically implies each other and (2) A's being is in some way the cause of B's being.

So far we have talked about the first condition, but what of the second? What kind of cause is Aristotle speaking about here? Aristotle himself is hesitant. He says that the prior item is only *in some way* a cause (*aition pōs*). Of course, in present-day terminology Aristotle speaks here about truth-making. However, I cannot think of any other passage where he says that the truth-making relation is an explanatory/causal relation or where he theorises about this relation.[57] I think it is simply underdetermined whether or not Aristotle thinks about one of the four causes here and, if so, which of them.

It remains for us to establish how the two descriptions of priority in nature relate to each other. If they are both criteria for the same kind of 'priority in

---

[56] I think that in Plato's account of the ontological priority of the form of the Good in *EE* I 8, 1217b2–15 we also encounter such a hybrid reading, since I take it that in the antecedent '*einai*' is best understood existentially, but in the consequent 'predicatively'. Due to limited space I cannot argue for this view in any detail here.

[57] I think that on the veridical reading, one might give a better account of the causal connection. One might claim that Aristotle says here that the object's being true is the efficient cause of the sentence's being true (and not the other way around). Why should we think here of an efficient cause? Arguably because one might think here about a property transferral. The object transfers its being true to the sentence.

nature', then they are each on their own sufficient but not necessary conditions for priority in nature. Their disjunction is a necessary and sufficient condition for priority in nature. If they are criteria for different kinds of 'priority in nature', then they are arguably each on their own necessary and sufficient conditions for the respective kind of priority in nature.

I think that they are criteria for the same kind of 'priority in nature'. There is just something which is ontological priority, but depending on the relata, this ontological priority can be captured in different ways. Nowhere does Aristotle suggest that he is speaking about different kinds of priority in nature.

2.5 Conclusion

In this section, I have argued that Aristotle puts forward a disjunctive account of priority in nature in *Cat.* 12 and 13 consisting of the following two conditions:

(1) A is ontologically prior to B if necessarily B's being implies A's being, but, not necessarily, A's being implies B's being.
(2) A is ontologically prior to B if necessarily A's being implies B's being, and necessarily B's being implies A's being, and A's being is a cause of B's being.

I have argued that 'implication of being' can be understood either existentially or predicatively in the special sense of 'being true' and that we even have 'mixed' readings (in which case two different uses of '*einai*' are employed in the same statement about priority). How one is to read the 'implication of being' must be decided on a case-by-case basis. I have explained why I both take a predicative reading of these passages to be problematic and take a special version of the predicative reading, namely an essentialist reading, to be unsatisfactory.

3 Ontological Priority and Simultaneity among Relatives in Aristotle's *Categories* 7

3.1 Introduction

In this section, I will argue that Aristotle also uses one of the criteria of the disjunctive account that he puts forward in *Cat.* 12 and 13, namely asymmetric implication of being, in *Cat.* 7.[58] In addition, I will contend that Aristotle proposes the following account of simultaneity in nature:

---

[58] Only Paula Gottlieb (1993) and John Cleary (1988) dedicate more detailed investigations to some of these passages. Gottlieb does so by closely examining Aristotle's account of perception and its relationship to his theory of relatives.

A and B are simultaneous in nature iff necessarily A's being implies B's being, and necessarily B's being implies A's being, and neither is the cause of the other.

3.2 Aristotle on Relatives

Aristotle's discussion of ontological dependencies among relatives cannot be understood without an understanding of his account of the nature of and reciprocity among relatives. As such, before we turn to the discussion of priority and simultaneity in nature in *Cat.* 7, it will be useful to highlight some crucial aspects of Aristotle's account of relatives. Note, however, that my two discussions (of Aristotle's theories of relativity in the *Categories* and *Metaphysics*, and of ontological dependencies in the *Categories*) remain independent. So whoever disagrees with my discussion of relativity might still accept my discussion of ontological dependencies and vice versa.

Aristotle's chapter on relatives is complex. From a present-day point of view, it is important to note that this chapter does not contain a discussion of relations as we find it in first-order logic or set theory.[59] The class of relatives is one among the ten categories of being.[60] Aristotle calls this category '*ta pros ti*' (τὰ πρός τι), which means 'items toward something'. However, there is much debate over what kind of items Aristotle is classifying under the heading of '*ta pros ti*'. He provides the following examples of relatives: double and half, slave and master, and knowledge and the knowable.

His metaphysics of relations in the *Categories* is difficult, because it is not always clear whether he is talking about the linguistic level or the ontological level. Many claim that Aristotle does not pay attention to the distinction between linguistic and ontological predication in the *Categories*. For nowhere does he make this difference explicit,[61] either because he was confused or, as Sedley suggests, because he takes the two to be co-extensive (Sedley, 2002: 333). Others argue that there is no clear evidence in the *Categories* that Aristotle thinks that, apart from the linguistically characterised items, there are extra-linguistic entities in the world that correspond to these items *in the case of relatives*.[62]

---

[59] Most importantly, Aristotle lacks the concept of a dyadic relation. See Hood (2004: 1–19) and Duncombe (2015: 13n19) for further discussion.

[60] In the *Categories* Aristotle introduces a tenfold division of beings – the ten categories: substance (e.g. man or horse); quantity (e.g. four feet); quality (e.g. the colour red); relatives (e.g. double); place (e.g. in the market); time (e.g. at noon); position (e.g. sitting); having (e.g. has gloves); doing (e.g. cutting); and being affected (e.g. being cut). See Studtmann (2014).

[61] See, for instance, Frede (1981); Malcolm (1981: 667); Sedley (2002: 333); Barnes (2007: 115–21).

[62] It is different as regards the other categories of being.

For our purposes, we need not solve this interpretative question. However, it is important to be alive to this difficulty. Consequently, we need to carefully distinguish several items in Aristotle's discussion on *ta pros ti*: relative/relational terms or predicates that are linguistic items; concrete relative items of which the relative predicates are predicated (for example, someone who is a slave[63]); and relative properties in virtue of which the concrete relative items are called relative. For example, Callias is a slave and called a 'slave' because of his having the property of being a slave.

In my view, Aristotle thinks that items belong to the class of *ta pros ti* insofar as a relation or relative predicates apply to them in a special way.[64]

In short, I think that Aristotle analyses one-place predicates, such as 'being a master' and 'being a slave', and investigates the nature of the items which they denote. He comes to the conclusion that to be a master is to stand in a specific relation to another being, namely a slave. By taking into account his linguistical investigations, he then classifies concrete relative items according to their way of standing in a relation to other items.[65] In my view, most of the time, Aristotle talks about concrete relative items. But this is, as I have said, controversial.

The other difficulty as regards Aristotle's treatment of relatives in the *Categories* is that he provides two different definitions of relatives, which pick out different sets of entities. I will not discuss these difficulties in any detail in this Element and would like to refer the interested reader to the works of Sedley (2002) on this issue. My own reading follows his.

---

[63] These can be primary substances or items in other categories, such as quantity.

[64] Cf. Morales (1994: 256). See also Studtmann (2014), who gives the following useful summary of this view: '[Aristotle] noticed that certain predicates in language are logically incomplete – they are not used in simple subject/predicate sentences of the form "a is F" but rather require some type of completion. To say "three is greater" is to say something that is incomplete – to complete it requires saying what three is greater than. Nonetheless, Aristotle accepted a doctrine according to which properties in the world always inhere in a single subject. In other words, although Aristotle countenanced relational predicates, and though he certainly thought that objects in the world are related to other objects, he did not accept relations as a genuine type of entity. So, Aristotle's category of relatives is a kind of halfway house between the linguistic side of relations, namely relational predicates, and the ontological side, namely relations themselves.'

[65] This view goes against the orthodox view which has, for instance, been defended by Ackrill (1963: 73: 'The categories classify things, not words') and Morales (1994: 257: 'In the *Categories* Aristotle is not classifying predicates, but the attributes or properties these stand for'). I think that his ontology of relatives is – at least in this respect – the same in both the *Categories* and the *Metaphysics*. However, recently a number of defences have been given of the view that Aristotle is concerned with concrete relative items rather than relational properties or predicates. In my view, Aristotle's 'stripping away' method in 7a22–b9 clearly speaks in favour of the view that when he discusses 'relatives', he is speaking about concrete relative items rather than relational properties. See also Duncombe (2020) and Hood (2004).

3.3 Simultaneity in Nature among Relatives in *Categories* 7 and 13

In *Cat.* 7 Aristotle provides the most extensive treatment of the accounts of simultaneity in nature and priority in nature in the *Categories* and *Metaphysics*. There he discusses ontological dependencies among relatives (discussion of simultaneity in nature among relatives (*Cat.* 7, 7b15–22) and discussion of priority in nature among relatives (*Cat.* 7, 7b22–8a12)).

In *Cat.* 7 Aristotle provides the following short yet dense discussion of simultaneity in nature among relatives:

> Relatives seem to be simultaneous by nature; and in most cases this is true. (1) For at the same time (*hama*) at which double is also half is, (2) and if half is, double is, and if slave is, master is; and similarly with the others. (3) Also, each carries the other to destruction (*sunanhairei allêla*); for if double is not half is not, and if half is not, double is not. So too with other such cases. (*Cat.* 7, 7b15–22.)

In this passage Aristotle makes three statements about simultaneity in nature whose relationship is not immediately clear: (1) being at the same time; (2) symmetric implication of being; and (3) symmetric destruction. Importantly, he adds in *Cat.* 13, 14b27–32 that a further condition for simultaneity must be fulfilled, namely that (4) neither of the relata is the cause of the other. I take this further condition to be implicit in *Cat.* 7, 7b15–22. This further condition must be added, since Aristotle claims that items whose being symmetrically depends upon each other and the one's being is the cause of the other's being stand in a priority in nature.

Depending on how one interprets these four statements, they are stronger or weaker signs/criteria for simultaneity in nature. On the weak reading, (1)–(4) are each on their own and jointly neither necessary nor sufficient conditions for simultaneity in nature. They are rather signs that serve as a guide for simultaneity in nature in many cases, but not in all cases. On the strong reading of (1)–(3), they are all logically equivalent and each of them jointly with (4) – i.e. (1)+(4); (2)+(4); and (3)+(4) – are necessary and sufficient conditions for simultaneity in nature.

I defend a hybrid version of the weak and strong readings. I argue that (1) is merely a sign for simultaneity in nature. In addition, I take (2) and (3) to be merely different formulations of the same criterion and, hence, logically equivalent. Assuming that (2) and (3) merely differ in description, I argue that both (2) jointly with (4) and (3) jointly with (4) are each necessary and sufficient conditions for simultaneity in nature.

There is a difficulty that needs to be tackled in order to decide whether to accept the weak reading, the strong reading, or the hybrid version, and that is whether we are entitled to ascribe to Aristotle the implicit use of modal operators in (1)–(4). I think that we are more entitled to ascribe an implicit use of modal operators in the formulation of (2) and (3), given some parallel passages, but not in the case of (1). For this reason, I defend the hybrid reading below.

3.3.1 Simultaneity in Time

Aristotle's first statement about simultaneity in nature reads as follows:

> Relatives seem to be simultaneous by nature; and in most cases this is true. (1) For at the same time (*hama*) at which double is also half is, […]. (*Cat.* 7, 7b15–17; transl. Ackrill, 1963.)

As in the previous discussions on ontological dependencies in *Cat.* 12 and 13, we need to understand whether 'double' (*diplasion*) and 'half' (*hemisu*) are subjects or predicates and how 'being' (*einai*) is to be interpreted.

As set out in subsection 3.2, I think that when Aristotle speaks of 'relatives', he mostly speaks about concrete relative items. I take him to be doing the same in this passage too. For this reason I take it that neither the predicative reading nor the existential-universal reading (discussed in the previous section) are viable options. Rather I take him to be talking about the temporal correlation among concrete relative items. To put it abstractly:

> Half and double are simultaneous in time since, at any time at which something that is a double exists, something that is a half exists; and at any time at which something that is a half exists, something that is a double exists.

In this reading, 'double' and 'half' are taken to be subjects and stand for concrete relative items. '*Einai*' is read existentially.

There remains the question of whether Aristotle implicitly uses the modal operator 'necessarily' (= strong reading) or not (= weak reading). This has a direct influence on the strength of this statement about simultaneity in nature.

On the weak reading of (1), Aristotle gives a *sign* or *mark* for simultaneity in nature but not a *criterion* (= necessary and/or sufficient condition).[66] For many things exist at the same time without being on the same ontological level. For example, let's assume that a flower acquires a particular shade of blue on 1

---

[66] The translation of '*hama*' as 'at the same time' is the most plausible reading, given that when Aristotle explains a little later that when two items do not exist *hama*, the one is prior *in time* to the other (*Cat.* 7, 7b22–7). And, as we will see, it is clear from his examples that he is talking about a temporal priority.

January 1912 which lasts exactly as it is until 31 December 2000. In addition, let's assume that Mary is born on 1 January 1912 and dies on 31 December 2000 at exactly the moment when the blue of the colour fades away. Just because Mary and the shade of blue exist at the same time, they are presumably not ontologically on the same level.

By contrast, if one thinks that Aristotle provides here a sufficient condition for priority and that he would not want to allow for all such cases to be cases of simultaneity in nature, one must take him to implicitly use the modal operator 'necessarily'. What supports this assumption is that Aristotle indeed regularly uses modal notions when speaking about dependence relations.[67] One might argue that here he was just careless and did not explicitly mention the necessity. Following this suggestion, the criterion is stronger. For all cases of accidental synchronic existence in time are excluded (such as the example noted above). The stronger version reads as follows:

> Necessarily, at any time A exists, B exists; and necessarily, at any time B exists, A exists.

On the strong reading, Aristotle gives a sufficient condition for simultaneity in nature.[68]

In sum, I have argued that there is a weak and a strong reading of (1). The weak reading is preferable, since it is the most natural reading and it functions as a good indicator for simultaneity in nature in the case of contingent entities. I think that the stronger reading reads too much into the passage, but I grant that it is a viable option.

3.3.2 Ontological Dependence: Symmetric Implication

In his second statement about simultaneity in nature, Aristotle says:

> Relatives seem to be simultaneous by nature; and in most cases this is true [...]; (2) and if half is, double is, and if slave is, master is; and similarly with the others. (*Cat.* 7, 7b15–19; transl. Ackrill, 1963.)

To put it abstractly, he says: 'If A is, then B is.' As it stands, I think that this conditional does not adequately represent Aristotle's idea. For in its current

---

[67] For instance, A can be without B, but B cannot be without A (*Metaph.* V 11 1019a1–4).

[68] The concern might be raised that even on the strong reading, too many things will turn out to be simultaneous in nature, since, for example, all necessarily existing entities will be ontologically on a par. I discuss this concern in Section 5.

form, the conditional does not represent a symmetry between A and B. However, such a symmetry is required because we are dealing with the simultaneity relation, which is necessarily symmetric. So I think we should read: 'If A is, B is, and if B is, A is.' I take it that adding the 'vice versa' is fairly uncontroversial, especially since we have symmetrical relations in the first and third statements about simultaneity in nature.

As explained earlier, since I take Aristotle to be talking about concrete relative items, I take 'double' and 'half' to be subjects of the conditional and '*einai*' to be read existentially. So, in my view, Aristotle makes the following statement about simultaneity in nature in this passage:

> If something that is a double exists, something that is a half exists; and if something that is a half exists, something that is a double exists.

Again, there are two readings of the statement above – a weak reading and a strong reading. On the weak reading, one reads the formulation as it stands. On this reading, it is only an indicator for priority but not yet a necessary and/or sufficient condition, since there is no *necessary* connection between A's and B's existence.

Defenders of the strong reading might argue that although Aristotle does not expressly mention the necessity, it is obviously to be understood as such. Note that in contrasting the items that are opposed as opposites from items that are opposed as relatives, Aristotle mentions the necessity explicitly (*Cat.* 11, 14a7). And when he mentions this criterion elsewhere, he also uses this modal operator or other modal operators, so one might argue that one is quite justified in making these additions (*Cat.* 12, 14a29–35; 13, 15a4–7. Cf. *Metaph.* V 11, 1019a1–4). For one is just making explicit what Aristotle might have taken as obviously to be understood. On the strong reading, Aristotle provides a sufficient condition for simultaneity in nature.[69] Since Aristotle does indeed quite frequently use modal operators in formulations of priority in nature, I think that in this case we should prefer the strong reading over the weak reading.

To put it abstractly, Aristotle says:

---

[69] Still, also on this strong reading, one needs to have a restricted account of implication if one wants to exclude the result that all necessary entities are ontologically on a par. The concern might be raised that although it might be desirable to have a more fine-grained account that is able to capture informative dependence relations among necessarily existing items, Aristotle is just unaware of this complication and his account only works for contingently existing items. I will briefly return to this issue in the final section. I argue that the discussion in *Gen. corr.* 337b14–337b24 suggests that Aristotle gives up on the analysis of ontological simultaneity and priority, in the strict sense, in terms of conditionals.

'Double' and 'half' are simultaneous in nature since, necessarily, $\exists x\ Dx \rightarrow$ $\exists y\ Hy$, and, necessarily, $\exists x\ Hx \rightarrow \exists y\ Dy$. (H = being half; D = being double.)

3.3.3 Ontological Dependence: Symmetric Destruction

In his third statement Aristotle says:

> Relatives seem to be simultaneous by nature; and in most cases this is true. [...] (3) Also, each carries the other to destruction (*sunanhairei allêla*); for if double is not half is not, and if half is not, double is not. So too with other such cases. (*Cat.* 7, 7b15–22.)

To put it abstractly:

(3) (If A is not, B is not) and (if B is not, A is not).

We need to understand what he means by 'symmetric destruction'. Note that Aristotle explains (*gar*) 'symmetric destruction' (*sunanhaireisthai allêla*) with 'symmetric non being' (*ouk einai*; *mê ontos*). Both notions plausibly have the same meaning.[70] For the reasons I have already given, I think that Aristotle speaks about concrete relative items and that '*einai*' should, hence, be read existentially. And again, although he does not mention the necessity explicitly, I take it to be implicit for the reasons given previously. On my reading, Aristotle says in this passage that:[71]

> Necessarily, if there does not exist something that is a double, there does not exist something that is a half; and, necessarily, if there does not exist something that is a half, there does not exist something that is a double.

Formalised, the dependence reads as follows:

> 'Double' and 'half' are simultaneous in nature since, necessarily, $\neg\exists x\ Dx \rightarrow$ $\neg\exists y\ Hy$ and, necessarily, $\neg\exists x\ Hx \rightarrow \neg\exists y\ Dy$. (H= being a half; D= being a double.)

As in the previous discussion, it must be emphasised that in the case of necessarily existing items, the third criterion in its current form is no good either, since according to the third criterion, all necessary items will turn out to be

---

[70] In my view, Aristotle explains a technical term of the Academy, namely the term '*anhaireisthai*', in ordinary Greek language by using '*einai*'.

[71] This is a case in which '*einai*' cannot mean 'to be essentially'. According to the essentialist reading, we would need to read: if the double is not essentially what it is, it follows that the half is not essentially what it is, and if the half is not essentially what it is, the double is not essentially what it is. This is not a plausible reading of the passage.

ontologically on a par, given that they cannot cease to exist. I will explore this concern in more detail in Section 5.

3.3.4 Interim Conclusion

In sum, Aristotle makes the following three statements about simultaneity in nature in *Cat.* 7, 7b15–22:

(1) A and B exist at the same time.
(2) Necessarily, A's existence and B's existence symmetrically imply each other.
(3) Necessarily, if A does not exist, B does not exist, and if B does not exist, A does not exist.

Importantly, (2) and (3) are deducible from each other and, hence, logically equivalent.[72] I call the dependence that is expressed by (2) and (3) a symmetric ontological dependence. Symmetric ontological dependence is a necessary condition for simultaneity in nature. If we read this statement together with a further condition on simultaneity in nature – namely that neither A's being nor B's being is the cause of the other – Aristotle provides a necessary and sufficient condition for priority in nature. (More on this further condition will follow in Section 3.3.5.)

Given that an indicator of simultaneity in nature between two entities is that they exist simultaneously in time, the second and third criteria of simultaneity in nature are best understood as a *symmetric necessary synchronic dependence.*[73] This can be formalised as follows:

> *A* and *B* symmetrically necessarily synchronically depend upon each other iff $\Box \forall t((\text{at } t\colon E(A)) \leftrightarrow (\text{at } t\colon E(B)))$.

This understanding of (2) and (3) is supported by the examples: the double necessarily *synchronically* exists with the half and the half necessarily *synchronically* exists with the double. In the same way, a slave necessarily *synchronically* exists with a master and a master necessarily *synchronically* exists with a slave. The examples do not stand in a relation of a symmetric necessary *past* or *future* dependence; rather they all stand in the relation of a symmetric necessary *synchronic* dependence.

I have provided both a weak and a strong reading for (1). If one accepts the weak reading, (1) is just an indicator for ontological simultaneity. By contrast,

---

[72] See *An. pr.* II 4, 57a36–57b18 on contraposition.
[73] See the discussion of the use of temporal operators in formulations of ontological dependence in sections 3.3.1 and 3.3.4.

if one accepts the strong reading, (1) is logically equivalent to (2) and (3). For if A and (1), then I can infer B and vice versa, hence (2) and (3).

If we take into account Aristotle's view on the nature of relatives, one can also account for why this symmetric ontological dependence holds. Given that the essence of half is entirely specified by its being in a relation to double, the half cannot exist without the double. And given that the essence of double is entirely specified by its being in a relation to half, the double cannot exist without the half.

3.3.5 A Further Condition on Simultaneity: No Causal Connection

In sum, I have so far argued that symmetric ontological dependence is a necessary condition for simultaneity in nature.

In *Cat.* 13, a chapter entirely dedicated to the discussion of 'simultaneity',[74] Aristotle takes up the discussion from *Cat.* 7 on simultaneity in nature:

> But those things are called simultaneous by nature which reciprocate as to implication of existence [sc. presupposition], provided that neither is in any way the cause of the other's existence, e.g. the double and the half. These reciprocate, since if there is a double there is a half and if there is a half there is a double, but neither is the cause of the other's existence. (*Cat.* 13, 14b27–32; transl. Ackrill, 1963.)

In this passage Aristotle again uses 'double' and 'half' as paradigmatic examples of a simultaneity in nature relation. As we have already seen in the discussion of *Cat.* 7, 'double' and 'half' are simultaneous in nature because they symmetrically necessarily synchronically existentially depend upon each other. Importantly, in the passage just cited, Aristotle notes that there holds only a simultaneity in nature relation *provided that neither is in any way the cause of the other's existence*. He mentions this addition again at the very end of *Cat.* 13:

> Thus we call simultaneous by nature those things that reciprocate as to implication of existence provided that neither is in any way the cause of the other's existence; [...]. (*Cat.* 13, 15a7–10; transl. Ackrill, 1963.)

This is an important addition. For Aristotle claims in *Cat.* 12 that if two items symmetrically imply each other and the being of one of the relata is in some sense a cause (*aition pōs*) of the being of the other item, then the item which is the cause is prior in nature to the caused item.[75]

---

[74] Apart from simultaneity in nature, Aristotle discusses simultaneity in time.

[75] *Cat.* 12, 14b9–23. See section 2.4.

In this way, Aristotle's account of simultaneity in nature relations in *Cat.* 13 further restricts the account of simultaneity in nature that he puts forward in *Cat.* 7. Putting the remarks in the two passages together, the new, more subtle account of simultaneity in nature that results reads as follows:

> A is simultaneous in nature (= simultaneous in substance) with B, if A and B symmetrically ontologically depend upon each other; and neither A's being is a cause of B's being nor B's being a cause of A's being.

It is striking that Aristotle mentions this further condition on simultaneity so late (only in *Cat.* 12 and 13) and not already in *Cat.* 7, where he extensively discusses simultaneity in nature.

By now turning to the discussion of priority in nature, we will see that the discussions on simultaneity relations proves to be helpful for understanding priority in nature relations in the *Categories*.

3.4 Priority in Nature among Relatives in *Categories* 7 and 12

3.4.1 I. Case Study in Categories 7: Knowledge and Its Object

In *Cat.* 7 Aristotle discusses two cases where there holds a priority in nature relation among relatives: (1) knowledge and its object; and (2) perception and its object. Aristotle argues in this passage that the knowable (*to epistêton*) and the perceptible (*to aisthêton*) are prior in nature to knowledge and perception respectively. In the following I will first discuss the knowledge case and then the perception case. He argues for the priority of the knowable over knowledge as follows:

> Yet it does not seem to be true of all relatives that they are simultaneous by nature. For the knowable would seem to be prior to knowledge. (1) For as a rule it is of actual things already existing (*prohyparchontōn*) that we acquire knowledge; in few cases, if any, could one find knowledge coming into being at the same time as what is knowable.

> (2) Moreover, destruction of the knowable carries knowledge to destruction, but knowledge does not carry the knowable to destruction. For if there is not a knowable there is not knowledge – there will no longer be anything for knowledge to be of – but if there is not knowledge there is nothing to prevent there being a knowable.

> Take, for example, the squaring of the circle, supposing it to be knowable; knowledge of it does not yet exist but the knowable itself exists.

> Again, if animal is destroyed there is no knowledge, but there may be many knowables. (*Cat.* 7, 7b22–35; transl. Ackrill, 1963.)

Aristotle gives two reasons why the knowable is prior in nature to knowledge:

(1) The knowable is prior in nature to knowledge because the knowable is *prior in time* to knowledge.[76] Aristotle claims that in most cases one acquires knowledge of a thing which exists already in actuality ('as a rule it is of actual things already existing (*prohyparchontôn*[77]) that we acquire knowledge').[78] The idea is that that which becomes an object of knowledge exists in actuality even before there are any subjects that perceive it. For example, Pythagoras' theorem existed *as a potential object of knowledge* even before Pythagoras proved it.

Aristotle claims that only in a few cases – if there are any such cases at all – do knowledge and the underlying item, insofar as it is a potential object of perception ('the knowable'), come into existence at the same time. One could argue that he thinks that, in most cases, knowledge and the thing known *as being known* do not exist at the same time, but the existence of the underlying item insofar as it is a potential object of perception precedes the knowledge in time. Since it is not the case that in all cases the prior in nature item exists prior in time, priority in time is an indicator rather than a necessary or sufficient condition for priority in nature. Since a great many things are prior in time to other entities, priority in time is a rather weak indicator of priority. It is so weak that one might want to drop it altogether.[79] There is a problem with Aristotle's discussion, namely that insofar as 'the knowable' is a potential object of knowledge, it depends upon there potentially existing other cognising subjects. Aristotle seems to be unaware of this problem.

(2) The second reason Aristotle gives for the priority in nature of the object of knowledge over knowledge is that whereas knowledge existentially depends upon the knowable, the knowable does not existentially depend upon knowledge of it.[80] Again, we find the terminology of an asymmetric destruction in the formulation of ontological priority: 'the destruction of the

---

[76] Note that I assume that Aristotle speaks here about knowledge in the strict sense of *scientific knowledge*. I think that the examples suggest this reading.

[77] The *prohyparchontôn* further supports the existential reading, for '*hyparchein*' is generally taken to mean 'to be already in existence'. See the entry on '*hyparchein*' in Liddell–Scott-Jones.

[78] *Cat.* 7b23–5; transl. Ackrill, 1963.

[79] Some Presocratic philosophers might have thought that priority in time just is necessary and sufficient for being ontologically prior, at least with some modifications: that which is at the beginning of the world is that which is most fundamental, like *nous* in the case of Anaxagoras or love and strife in the case of Empedocles. See Menn (2009).

[80] Cf. Hood (2004: 67).

knowable (*episthêton anhaireton*) destroys simultaneously (*sunanhairei*) the knowledge, but the destruction of the knowledge does not simultaneously destroy the knowable'.[81] As in his discussions on simultaneity in nature, Aristotle uses '*anhaireisthai*' (to destruct) as a technical term. For now he explains '*anhaireisthai*' in terms of not-being (*mê einai*; 7b29–31).[82] Since I think that '*anhaireisthai*' means 'to go out of existence *simpliciter*', we should take 'being' (*einai*) to have the same meaning.[83] Recall that given that Aristotle arguably speaks here of concrete relative items, neither the predicative nor the existential-universal reading are viable options.

I suggest further qualifying Aristotle's account of ontological priority, although he does not make this refinement explicit. In the discussion on simultaneity in nature, I argued that we should conceive of simultaneity in nature as a symmetric *synchronic* necessary dependence, rather than as a symmetric *past* necessary dependence. In my view, we should conceive of priority in nature as a non-symmetric *synchronic* necessary dependence. For arguably knowledge depends *synchronically* upon the knowable, but not the other way around. Indeed, by using the expression '*sunanhairein*' (destroy together with), Aristotle might highlight that the posterior item is destroyed *at the same time* (*hama* = *sun*) as the prior item is destroyed.[84] Hence, I suggest the following reconstruction:

> A is prior in nature to B iff
>
> $\Box \forall t((\text{at } t: \neg\ E(A)) \rightarrow (\text{at } t: \neg\ E(B)))$ and $\neg\Box\forall t((\text{at } t: \neg\ E(B)) \rightarrow (\text{at } t: \neg\ E(A)))$.
>
> Necessarily, B does not exist at a time unless A exists at that time, but it is not the case that necessarily A does not exist at a time unless B exists at that time.

Aristotle provides two examples to illustrate his view that the knowable is asymmetrically existentially independent from knowledge. The first example is the squaring of the circle. For the sake of argument, he supposes that the squaring of the circle is possible.[85] He points out that knowledge of the squaring of the circle, i.e. its proof (= actual knowledge), so far does not exist; however,

---

[81] Cf. *EE* I 8, 1217b2–15; *Cat.* 7, 7b15–22; and *Metaph.* XIII 8, 1083b–33.

[82] Cf. *Cat.* 7, 7b15–22 and *Metaph.* XIII 8, 1083b–33.

[83] A predicative reading or an essentialist reading of '*einai*' in this passage is implausible.

[84] See the entry in Liddell–Scott–Jones: 'destroy together with', 'τινά τινι' Isoc. *Ep.* 2.3, Plb. 5.11.5, etc.; 'τι ἅμα τινι' Id.6.46.7; simply destroy at the same time, Phld. *Mus.* VIII 148 fr. 10.

[85] In Aristotle's time, it was not clear whether it would be possible to prove the squaring of the circle.

assuming that a proof of it is possible, the underlying object insofar as it is a *possible* object of knowledge (= 'the knowable') already exists.

The second illustration of the existential priority of the object of knowledge over knowledge is more complicated. Aristotle says: 'Again, if animal is destroyed there is no knowledge, but there may be many knowables' (7b33–5). This is a rather cryptic remark. I think that Aristotle aims to highlight that knowledge, in contrast to the knowables, existentially depends upon a subject of knowledge. For without a subject of knowledge, there is no knowledge.[86]

However, this claim is problematic because if it is not possible that a cognising subject exists, the substrate of knowledge *as being knowable* does not exist either. It might continue to exist in its own nature, but not *as being knowable*. For example, the theorem of Pythagoras *as* mathematical theorem might still exist as a state of affairs if it were *impossible* that there are cognising subjects in the cosmos, but not as a potential object of knowledge. For it could only exist as a potential object of knowledge if knowledge of it were possible, but in a world in which there are no cognising subjects (and of necessity so), it is not a possible object of knowledge.[87]

In sum, on my reading, the ontological priority of the object of knowledge over knowledge consists in an asymmetrical necessary existential dependence. Aristotle thinks that the necessary existential dependence that holds between the two relata is explained by the essences of the relata. I take it that, according to Aristotle, P is part of what it is to be knowledge of P. For example, the fact that 2+2=4 is part of what it is to be knowledge of the fact that 2+2=4. Hence, the knowledge of P is asymmetrically essentially dependent upon the object of knowledge P. This asymmetrical essential dependence explains why the asymmetrical existential dependence holds.

My reconstruction of the second criterion poses a problem, since it requires counterpossibles in cases where at least one of the relata necessarily exists, and we still do not have a satisfactory semantics for counterpossibles, and Aristotle presumably does not have one either. However, from many passages it is clear that Aristotle is often intentionally engaging in counterpossible reasoning and that he often does so in order to determine dependence relations among entities.[88]

---

[86] Compare this discussion with the discussion of the dependence of time upon soul in *Ph.* 223a21–9.

[87] Things are further complicated by the fact that for Aristotle some cognising subjects exist by necessity (the unmoved movers).

[88] See, for instance, *Cael.* IV 3, 310b2–5, where he investigates the motion of the four simple bodies in a counterpossible scenario, and *Ph.* 23a21–9, where he openly engages in counterpossible reasoning in order to determine the nature of time. See also the stripping argument in *Metaph.* VII 3, 1029a10–27 and *Metaph.* VII 15, 1040a29–33, where Aristotle suggests that the

From these passages it is clear that Aristotle intentionally uses counterpossibles and that he arguably thinks that not all of them are trivially true. So he must have some theoretical grasp of what makes them true and what makes them false, and this is presumably tightly connected with his view of how the relata are essentially related.

What is surprising, then, is that even though Aristotle has the requisite tools to restrict the account of ontological dependence understood in existential terms, he does not use them.

For whatever reason, he does not seem to recognise the need to restrict the account, despite his being aware of its complications. This is particularly puzzling since his employment of counterpossibles requires exactly these additional resources and is sensitive to the kinds of distinctions that cannot be captured by existential implication that he is arguably using in his account of ontological priority.

3.4.2 II. Case Study in Categories 7: Perception and Its Object

Let us now turn to Aristotle's second case of priority in nature in *Cat.* 7. It concerns the ontological relation between perception and its object. We find that Aristotle also uses the same criterion for ontological priority in this case, namely *asymmetric existential dependence*. In addition, I argue that Aristotle's discussion is particularly interesting for understanding his criticism of the Protagorean position that 'man is the measure of all things'. For although Aristotle agrees with Protagoras that perception and the objects of perception are relatives, he argues – against Protagoras – that the objects of perception are existentially independent of a perceiver.

In *Cat.* 7, 7b35–8a12 Aristotle argues that the perceptible and perception also stand in the relation of priority in nature. His discussion can only be properly understood on the basis of his theory of perception. As such, I will offer a brief sketch of it here, insofar as it is important for our discussion.

In several works, especially in the *De Anima*, in which Aristotle analyses the functions and capacities of the soul, he is arguing against a naive account of perception. He says that many Presocratic philosophers believe that without there being a subject actually perceiving an object, there exist no colours and other perceptible qualia. ('The earlier students of nature were mistaken in their view that without sight there was no white or black, without taste no savour'

---

sun might stop moving, or consider *Cael.* 1 2, 269a2–9, where he investigates the impossible situation in which *aether* is moved by force non-circularly.

(*De an.* III 2, 426a29).[89]) In addition, we know from Plato's *Theaetetus* and from discussions in *Metaphysics* IV that Protagoras holds a very similar view. According to Protagoras, the perceiver is the measure of the perceived object. The Presocratic and Protagorean view has the implausible consequence that the object of perception ceases to exist as soon as a perceiver stops actually perceiving it.[90]

In contrast to the Presocratics and Protagoras, Aristotle argues that even without there being a subject actually perceiving the object of perception, there exists already in actuality an item as a potential object of perception. For example, the green apple on the table will not cease – neither completely nor as being green and sweet (and thus perceptible) – as soon as I stop looking at it or eating it.

In *De an.* III 2, Aristotle clarifies the relations between a perception and a perceptible by introducing a distinction between actuality (*energeia*) and potentiality/capacity (*dunamis*):

> The activity of the sensible object and that of the sense is one and the same activity, and yet the distinction between their being remains. Take as illustration actual sound and actual hearing: a man may have hearing and yet not be hearing, and that which has a sound is not always sounding. But when that which can hear is actively hearing and that which can sound is sounding, then the actual hearing and the actual sound come about at the same time (these one might call respectively harkening and sounding). [...] Since the actualities of the sensible object and of the sensitive faculty are one actuality in spite of the difference between their modes of being, actual hearing and actual sounding appear and disappear from existence at one and the same moment, and so actual savour and actual tasting, etc., while as potentialities one of them may exist without the other. (*De an.* III 2, 425b25–426a1; 426a15–25; transl. Smith, 1931.)

In this passage Aristotle first draws a distinction between the actual exercise of a capacity and the capacity itself. He provides two examples: (1) actually hearing a sound and being capable of hearing a sound; and (2) actually making a sound and being capable of making a sound. Aristotle claims that the actual hearing of a sound and the actual making of a sound necessarily take place simultaneously in time.[91] In my view, Aristotle is even committed to the

---

[89] Transl. Smith, 1931. Cf. *Metaph.* IX 3, 1047a4–7 (Aristotle on the Megarians): 'It is the same too as regards inanimate things. For there will be no cold or hot or sweet or in general anything perceptible if things are not being perceived; so it will turn out that they assert the view of Protagoras.' (Transl. Makin, 2006.)

[90] For a discussion of this, see Gottlieb (1993).

[91] In 426a24–5 Aristotle makes clear that he is talking about a necessary dependence.

stronger existential dependence, namely that it is not possible that actual sounding exists without the actual hearing and conversely.[92] Hence, apart from the necessary simultaneity in time, there is a simultaneity in nature relation between the actual sounding and the actual hearing.

He claims that, by contrast, there are no such simultaneities in time and in nature when it comes to the capacities, i.e. the potential objects of perception. For there to exist an entity capable of being heard, it is not necessary that there exists a being actually hearing it.[93]

After this brief introduction to Aristotle's theory of perception, let us turn to his account of the ontological dependencies among these entities in the *Categories*. On my reading, in *Cat.* 7, 7b35–8a12 Aristotle argues that the object of perception is asymmetrically existentially independent from actual perceptions of it. He says:

> The case of perception is similar to this [sc. the knowledge example]; for the perceptible seems to be prior [sc. in nature] to perception. (1) For the destruction of the perceptible carries perception to destruction, but perception does not carry the perceptible to destruction. For perceptions are to do with body and in body, and if the perceptible is destroyed, body too is destroyed (since body is itself a perceptible), and if there is not body, perception too is destroyed; hence the perceptible carries perception to destruction. But perception does not carry the perceptible. For if animal is destroyed perception is destroyed, but there will be something perceptible, such as body, hot, sweet, bitter, and all the other perceptibles.
>
> (2) Moreover, perception comes into existence at the same time as what is capable of perceiving – an animal and perception come into existence at the same time – but the perceptible exists even before perception exists; fire and water and so on, of which an animal is itself made up, exist even before there exists an animal at all, or perception. Hence the perceptible would seem to be prior to perception. (*Cat.* 7, 7b35–8a12.)

Aristotle gives two reasons as to why the perceptible is prior in nature to perception.

(1) The perceptible is prior to perception because there holds an asymmetric existential dependence between the perceptible and the perception. (2) The

---

[92] This can be explained by his theory of change. I will not argue for this claim in this book.

[93] One might read the claim 'But this is not necessary for those things spoken of in terms of potentiality' differently. One might think that Aristotle claims that for there to exist an entity capable of being heard, it is not necessary that there exists an entity capable of making sound. However, this reading is rather implausible. For if it is not possible that there exists a being capable of hearing, it is not possible that there is sound (because there is no being capable of making sound).

perceptible is prior in nature to perception because it exists prior in time to perception. Whereas *asymmetric existential dependence* is a necessary and sufficient condition for priority in nature, *priority in time* is merely an indicator for priority in nature.

Regarding (1): Aristotle's discussion in the *De an.* now helps us to understand better the ontological dependence relations between perceptions and perceptibles in this passage. While there holds a simultaneity in nature relation between an actual perception and an actually perceived item, there holds a priority relation between an actual perception and a potentially perceived item. In *Cat.* 7 Aristotle is concerned with the latter dependence relation. He says that if the underlying subject is destroyed (which implies that all its perceptible qualities are gone), the perception of this item (and even the possibility of its perception) is destroyed too. By contrast, it is not the case that if the actual perception of an item ceases to exist, the item at which the perception is directed ceases to exist as well. Again, I take it that, as in the previous cases, although Aristotle does not mention the necessity of the dependence explicitly, this is to be understood.

The best way to capture this relation is, again (as in the case of knowledge and its object), in terms of an asymmetric necessary existential dependence: necessarily, if P does not exist at a time, the perception of P does not exist at a time, but not necessarily, if the perception of P does not exist at a time, P does not exist at that time.[94]

Regarding (2): Aristotle's second justification of the priority of the perceptible is more complicated. He claims that the perceptible is prior in nature to perception because the perceptible is *prior in time* to perception. It is noteworthy that this account is crucially different from the account of the priority in time of the knowable over the object of knowledge. For Aristotle does not argue that the object of perception is simply prior in nature because it exists prior in time to the perception of it, as he did in the case of the knowledge example. Aristotle's argument is more complicated here, and runs as follows:

(1) Perception and animals come into existence at the same time.
(2) The material constituents of an animal exist before the animal.
(3) The material constituents of an animal are perceptibles.
(4) Hence, some perceptibles exist before perception.

---

[94] Importantly, Aristotle's account of the priority of the perceptible ultimately breaks down. For *qua being an object of perception* the underlying object depends upon the possibility of the existence of a subject of perception. If it is not possible that there is a subject of perception, the object in question is no potential object of knowledge. That is why I think that this account is unsatisfactory in the end. A further problem in Aristotle's discussion is that he does not clearly distinguish between tokens and types, and we do not know how to individuate perceptions. I take it that he speaks here about token perceptions, but nowhere does he explicitly say so.

The point of the argument is to show that the object of perception is prior in time to the perception. Aristotle starts by claiming that the subject of perception and the perception come into being at the same time. A rationale for this claim might be that living beings, which are, according to Aristotle, the only beings capable of perceiving, start to perceive as soon as they start to live. For Aristotle, living and perceiving necessarily synchronically depend upon each other. Then Aristotle claims that animals are made up of elements, which exist before the animal and continue to exist after the animal, so these elements are prior. The elements in question are by themselves perceptibles. Hence, given that animals and perception come into existence at the same time and animals are made up of perceptibles, perceptibles are prior in time to perception.

In sum, on my reading, Aristotle argues in *Cat.* 7, 7b22–8a12 that at least some relatives stand in a priority in nature relation. He discusses two exemplary cases: (1) knowledge and its object; (2) perception and its objects. Priority in time is an indicator for priority in nature, and asymmetric necessary existential dependence is a sufficient condition for priority in nature.

3.5 Conclusion

In this section, I have analysed Aristotle's account of *simultaneity in nature* and *priority in nature* in *Cat.* 7. Both are central for understanding the structure of reality that Aristotle constructs in his *Categories*.

I have argued that Aristotle proposes an account of *simultaneity* in nature which captures a symmetric ontological dependence. On my reading, Aristotle puts forward an indicator for when two entities are simultaneous in nature, namely that both entities *exist at the same time*. In addition, he submits a necessary and sufficient condition for simultaneity in nature, which reads as follows:

> A and B are simultaneous in nature iff necessarily A's being implies B's being and B's being implies A's being and neither's being is the cause of the other.[95]

Moreover, I have argued that Aristotle puts forward an indicator for priority in nature, which is priority in time, and makes use of the previously discussed sufficient condition, namely:

---

[95] If one accepts my suggestion to add temporal operators, the account reads as follows: *A* and *B* are simultaneous in nature iff $\Box \forall t((\text{at } t: E(A)) \leftrightarrow (\text{at } t: E(B)))$, and neither's being is the cause of the other.

A is ontologically prior to B if necessarily B's being implies A's being, but not necessarily, A's being implies B's being.[96]

Since the relata of the priority and simultaneity relations are concrete relative items, '*einai*' should be understood existentially in the above accounts of simultaneity and priority in nature. I have explained why I take an essentialist reading to be unsatisfactory.

It is notable that in the *Categories* all dependencies in the cases of simultaneity and priority in nature are cases where the dependence is synchronic. By contrasting priority with simultaneity, I was able to strengthen my claim that most probably Aristotle implicitly operates with temporal operators in cases where the relata exist in time, so that we need to distinguish between different temporal existential dependencies in order to capture the relevant relations.[97]

4 The Primacy of Primary Substances in Aristotle's *Categories*

4.1 Introduction

Most interpreters of the *Categories* argue that the primacy of the primary substances consists in their ontological priority over secondary substances and items in other categories. They base their view on a controversial passage in which Aristotle claims that secondary substances and beings in other categories depend upon primary substances (*Cat.* 5, 2b3–6). A crucial assumption of their interpretation is that the dependence between primary substances and other beings is asymmetrical.[98] I argue that we should drop this assumption. In this passage Aristotle commits himself only to the view that items in other categories and secondary substances existentially depend upon primary substances; he does not also commit himself to the view that primary substances do not existentially depend upon secondary substances and items in other categories. I propose that Aristotle argues elsewhere in the *Categories* that the primacy of primary substances consists in their being a subject for the other entities. Hence, in my view, he does not establish their primacy by appealing to their ontological priority.

---

[96] Adding temporal operators, this reads: *A* is prior in nature to *B* if $\Box \forall t((\text{at } t: E(B)) \rightarrow (\text{at } t: E(A)))$ and $\neg \Box \forall t((\text{at } t: E(A)) \rightarrow (\text{at } t: E(B)))$.

[97] Elsewhere, I argue that we have reason for thinking that in the *Metaphysics* Aristotle uses at least one case of priority in nature where the priority is understood in terms of an asymmetric existential *past* dependence. (I am thinking about the priority in nature of the eternal substances over the perishable substances in *Metaph.* IX 8 and XII.) This suggests that the relationship as regards ontological priority in the *Categories* and in the *Metaphysics* is more complex than has been thought until now.

[98] Recall that in my use of the notion 'dependence', it is not necessarily asymmetric.

4.2 *Categories* 5, 2b3–6

In the *Categories* Aristotle introduces a fourfold division of types of being. He believes that there are two different ways in which an attribute can belong to a subject: it can be predicated of a subject or be in a subject.[99] Taking these two modes as parameters, we get the following division: primary substances (property-bearing individuals, e.g. Socrates, which are neither in a subject nor said of a subject), accidental universals (which are said of and in a subject), accidental particulars (which are not said of but are in a subject – they are unique to the individual substances in which they inhere and not repeatable), and secondary substances (which are said of a subject but not in a subject).

In a controversial passage – one of the most discussed passages in the entire *Categories* – Aristotle claims that secondary substances and beings in other categories depend upon primary substances (*prôtai ousiai*):

> All the other things are either said of the primary substances as subjects or in them as subjects. This is clear from an examination of cases. For example, animal is predicated of man and therefore also of the individual man; for were it predicated of none of the individual men it would not be predicated of man at all. Again, colour is in body and therefore also in an individual body; for were it not in some individual body it would not be in body at all. Thus all the other things are either said of the primary substances as subjects or in them as subjects. So if the primary substances were not, it would be impossible for any of the other things to be. (*Cat.* 5, 2a34–2b6; transl. Ackrill, 1963.)[100]

In this passage Aristotle discusses how primary substances relate to secondary substances and items in other categories. There are two different readings of this passage: an asymmetrical reading and a neutral reading. If we read *Cat.* 5, 2b3–6 carefully in its context, we see that Aristotle makes an inference in this passage by introducing the conditional formulation with a 'so' ('*oun*'). For Aristotle claims in *Cat.* 5, 2b3–6 that an ontological dependence of secondary substances, accidental particulars, and accidental universals *follows from* the fact that the primary substances are their subjects or hosts.

---

[99] *Cat.* 2, 1b3–6. On the difficulties of understanding Aristotle's classification of being, see the first subsections of Sections 3.1 and 3.2. For further discussion, see Ackrill (1963: 75), Moravcsik (1967: 83), and, recently, Kohl (2008: 153).

[100] There is a textual problem. Aristotle repeats lines 2b3–6a with a few slight modifications after 2b6a. I follow the *communis opinio* by taking the repetition to be a mere dittography. Also Ackrill, for instance, does not translate 2b6b–c. The dittography has already been noted by Simplicius *In Cat.* (88, 25–30). Minio-Paluello prints the repetition (without placing them in parentheses) but notes that: '6b–c verba *panta... einai* dittographiam arbitratus expungenda esse dixit Simplicius, quem editores omnes secuti sunt' Aristotle and Minio-Paluello, 1956: 7).

Questions remain as to what consequences he is drawing from the previous discussion and, in particular, how we are to interpret the conditional.

According to the neutral reading, which to date has only been advanced by Duerlinger (1970), Aristotle here commits himself only to the view that items in other categories and secondary substances existentially depend upon primary substances, and does not also commit himself to the view that primary substances do not existentially depend upon secondary substances and items in other categories.

By contrast, according to the asymmetrical reading, Aristotle commits himself to the view that items in other categories ontologically depend upon primary substances, whereas primary substances do not ontologically depend upon items in other categories.

The defenders of the asymmetrical reading disagree, though, over how to interpret the argument because they disagree over how to interpret the priority in nature relation. According to the existential interpretation of the priority in nature relation, proposed by Ackrill and widely accepted,[101] Aristotle claims in this passage that primary substances are primary because they can *exist without* secondary substances and items in other categories, whereas secondary substances and items in other categories cannot exist without the primary substances. By contrast, according to the essentialist reading of the priority in nature relation, which is very popular among Neo-Aristotelian interpreters of this passage,[102] the dependence relation in question is an *asymmetric essential dependence*: whereas the items in other categories and the secondary substances essentially depend upon the primary substances, the primary substances do not essentially depend upon them. A prominent way to spell out what an essential dependence consists in is Michail Peramatzis' reading. According to Peramatzis, Aristotle claims in this passage that a primary substance is prior in nature to its accidents because a determinate subject, a particular substance, makes its accidents what they are, but the accidents do not make the subject what it is. For 'non-substance attributes or accidental compounds depend, for their nature as qualifying-beings, on particular substances having them as qualifications' (Peramatzis, 2011: 244).

In sum, defenders of the asymmetrical interpretation assume that Aristotle implicitly makes a claim about priority in nature and an asymmetrical claim in this passage.

---

[101] Ackrill (1963: 83); Moravcsik (1967: 95); Loux (1991: 16).

[102] In recent Neo-Aristotelian discussions, as well as in historical studies on Aristotle's metaphysics, this passage has been discussed extensively: Lowe (2009); Corkum (2008); Koslicki (2013); Peramatzis (2011).

In what follows, I want to defend the neutral reading. I argue that even without ascribing an asymmetrical claim to Aristotle, his assertion (namely that the other beings cannot exist without primary substances) is intelligible, interesting, and – in the philosophical context in which he is writing – highly challenging. On this reading, Aristotle can be seen as distancing himself from Platonic metaphysics.[103] For Plato does not think that universals or other kinds of entities – such as the objects of mathematics – existentially depend upon primary substances.

This, however, presents us with a conundrum. Given that Aristotle only says in this passage that the secondary substances and the items in other categories cannot be without the primary substances, and given that he does not make the further claim that the primary substances can be without the secondary substances and the items in the other categories, why do most interpreters think that he is also committed to this further claim? Here is my charitable hypothesis: they want to explain the primacy of the primary substances and they think that primary substances are primary because they are prior in nature to items in other categories. Now, there is a good reason why most interpreters hitherto have taken Aristotle to be talking about priority in nature in this passage: it seems that he is simply stating the first part of a common formulation of priority in nature, which he formulates in several passages in the *Categories* and in the *Metaphysics* as follows:[104]

> A is prior in nature to B if, if A were not, B would not be, but it is not the case that if B were not, A would not be.

Interpreters of *Cat.* 5, 2b3–6 have seen the structural similarities between this formulation of priority in nature and the dependence claim that Aristotle makes in 2b3–6. It looks as if he mentions the first part of the priority formulation (if A were not, B would not be) and then takes the second part of the priority formulation (if B were not, A would not be) to be implied.[105]

Because they want to explain the primacy of the primary substances, they read more into the text than what Aristotle actually wrote. They would find the neutral reading to be inadequate, because there is a gap in Duerlinger's interpretation: Duerlinger does not provide an account for the primacy of the primary substances. In the following, I argue that defenders of the asymmetrical

---

[103] Duerlinger (1970).

[104] *Cat.* 7, 7b22–8a12; 12, 14a29–35; 13, 14b24–15a12; *Metaph.* V 11, 1019a1–4.

[105] Defenders of an existential and essentialist interpretation merely disagree over how to interpret 'being' ('*einai*') in this passage. Whereas 'being' is read as 'existence' on the existential reading, 'being' is understood as 'being what it is' on the essentialist reading.

reading do not close this gap either, i.e. they do not provide convincing accounts of the primacy of the primary substances.

Now, if those who interpret Aristotle as making this asymmetrical claim in 2b3–6 could make a good case for their reading by showing that the asymmetrical reading makes good sense and that all senses of priority and primacy are the same, then their reading would be an attractive one. However, as I will demonstrate in the following three subsections, no defender of this view – even if several, rather distinct, interpretations of the priority have been proposed – can make a good case for the asymmetrical reading.

In the final observations, I claim that Aristotle does not argue for the primacy of primary substances in this passage and that, generally, priority in nature does not account for the primacy of primary substances. Aristotle makes clear that the primacy of the primary substances consists in their being subjects for all other items.

4.3 A Problem for Both Interpretations: The Secondary Substances

The most serious argument against the asymmetrical accounts is that primary substances do depend ontologically (in terms of both existence and essence) upon secondary substances and beings in the other categories. For (1) primary substances existentially depend upon secondary substances and at least some accidents for their own existence (Socrates cannot exist without having a colour, for instance); and (2) the secondary substances are essentially prior to the primary substances, because they are mentioned in the definition of primary substances ('living being' is part of the definition of Socrates, for example). Thus we do not achieve the required asymmetry.

Some defenders of the existential and essentialist interpretations try to avoid this problem by excluding the secondary substances as relata of the priority relation. They claim that Aristotle is concerned here only with the relation between the primary substances and items in other categories.

There are two problems with this reply. First, from the context it is fairly clear that Aristotle includes the secondary substances among the items that are dependent upon the primary substances. He refers to items of different ontological status (he says 'any of the other things' <*ti tôn allôn*)) when he mentions the dependent items, so he includes secondary substances and accidental universals among these (2b6). Note that he uses 'animal' (*zôon*) as one of the examples of items that are predicated and this is one of his standard examples for secondary substances (2a35–8). As such, it is very difficult to read it as not referring to secondary substances, although he does not mention the word secondary substances explicitly in 2a34–2b6. That he indeed refers to all three kinds of entities that are different from beings that are neither in nor predicated of anything is further supported by the fact that he discusses all three of them in the previous passage.

Second, the things to which the primary substances should be prior are the secondary substances. Aristotle is giving us an ordering when he speaks of primary and secondary substances, so the primary substances should be prior to the secondary substances. But neither of the previous interpretations can account for this ordering.

4.4 Primacy as Asymmetric Existential Dependence?

According to the asymmetrical existential reading of this passage, Aristotle commits himself to the view that primary substances can exist without secondary substances and items in other categories.[106]

I have already argued that this reading is problematic, since it seems that the primary substances cannot exist without the secondary substances. The existential dependence between the primary and secondary substances is mutual, so the asymmetrical existential reading of the conditional cannot be correct.[107] I will now argue that an existential priority of the primary substances over accidents also seems problematic.

The following objection can be raised against such an interpretation. On the assumption that he thinks that there cannot be bare particulars, we do not get the required asymmetry, because primary substances cannot exist without any accidental particulars (items that are 'in' primary substances, but not said of them).[108] In *Metaph.* VII 3, for instance, Aristotle argues that bare prime matter is impossible (1029a12–21). This argument could also be said to cover bare particulars. In addition, in the *Physics* Aristotle considers the possibility of a bare particular and says that it is absurd (*Ph.* I 2, 185a20–32). Even if one does not import findings from the *Metaphysics* and the *Physics*, there is no support in the *Categories* for the view that there can be bare particulars. Paradigmatic examples of primary substances are ordinary objects, such as Socrates or Callias. Now, neither Socrates nor Callias could exist without being human (a secondary substance) nor without having a colour (a quality) or being in some place or other (a place). Nowhere does Aristotle mention the possibility of bare

---

[106] Ackrill (1963: 83); Moravcsik (1967: 95); Loux (1991: 16).

[107] Ackrill himself points out that the reading is problematic (1963: 83).

[108] *Cat.* 2, 1a23–9. See Theodore Sider's (2006) clarifications of the notion 'bare particular'.

particulars. This suggests that there is no such thing as a bare particular in Aristotle's ontology in the *Categories*. All his examples are particular substances that are qualified in a number of ways.

In light of this difficulty, the original existential interpretation has been modified. According to the modified reading, Aristotle only claims in this passage that primary substances are prior to accidental particulars in that they can exist without accidental particulars taken distributively, but not taken collectively. For example, Socrates can exist without this specific colour, but not without any colour.[109] This reading has been defended, for instance, by Gisela Striker. She says: 'However the difficulty with differentiae or essential attributes is to be solved, we might agree that particular contingent attributes do depend on their subjects for their existence, since it is possible for a subject to exist without having them, but not vice versa. So while it is not possible for a thing to have no attributes at all, it is possible for a subject to change its attributes while remaining the same, but not for a particular attribute to change subject. If one thinks of attributes in the context of change, as Aristotle evidently does in this passage, one can at least understand his view about their dependent status.'[110]

The modified reading is also subject to several difficulties:

(1) The modified reading does not give an account of why we should take the secondary substances to be excluded, although they are evidently among the relata. For instance, Striker claims that 'the species and the genera of substances are included in "all the others"' (Striker, 2011: 145–6). Yet at the same time she claims that to include them among the relata leads to a 'dismally failed argument'. So they ought not be counted among the relata.

(2) Primary substances will be ontologically on a par with some accidental particulars even on the modified account. For there will be a symmetrical dependence between primary substances and *propria* (= necessary individualised non-replicable accidents). This is because it is both the case that (1) necessarily if Socrates exists, his capacity for laughing exists, and (2) necessarily if Socrates' capacity for laughing exists, Socrates exists. The relation between substance and *propria* is thus mistakenly classified as being symmetrical. Accordingly, we do not arrive at the required asymmetry.

---

[109] See also Koslicki's (2013) and Lowe's (2009) treatment of the different versions of an existential dependence.

[110] Striker (2011: 145–6). According to Striker, Aristotle accounts for the priority of the primary substances over the secondary substances in a different way. According to Striker, both the primary and the secondary substances are called substances, since they are both subjects. Yet the primary substances are primary, since only they satisfy the conditions of being a 'certain this' (*tode ti*) – a condition which Aristotle claims to be characteristic of substance (*Cat.* 5, 3b10).

One might reply to these objections in the following way. Aristotle offers a further account for priority in nature in cases of reciprocal existential entailment in *Cat.* 12: he claims that in such cases, the entity which is in some way the cause or explanation (*pôs aition*) of the other entity is prior (*Cat.* 12, 14b9–24). Taking into consideration this further account of priority in nature, we do get asymmetrical relations in the previous counterexample. Socrates seems to be grounding his capacity for laughing and thus turns out to be prior to his capacity for laughing.

The problem with this reply is that if we appeal to Aristotle's second account of priority in nature in the *Categories*, it is not the existential independence of primary substances from their accidental attributes that accounts for their primacy. But the central point of both the original and the modified existential interpretation was meant to be that the primacy of primary substances is accounted for by their asymmetrical existential independence from the secondary substances and items in other categories. In addition, there will be ways in which the secondary substances and even accidents are in some way explanatory and causes (*pôs aition*) of the primary substances. So again, we might not get the required asymmetry.

In sum, I have shown why the two versions of the existential interpretation are problematic. If they want to ascribe this asymmetrical claim to Aristotle, they must make a better case for their reading.

4.5 Primacy as Asymmetric Essential Dependence?

In view of the difficulties facing existential interpretations, different essentialist interpretations have been offered. As with the existential readings, defenders of the essentialist reading maintain that Aristotle is making an asymmetrical claim in this passage. However, they differ insofar as they read '*ousôn*' and '*einai*' in 2b5–6 as 'to be what it is' (whereas defenders of the existential interpretation read it as 'to exist').

Defenders of an essentialist reading claim that primary substances are prior to items that belong to other categories because they are essentially prior to them. They are essentially prior in that they determine their identity. Versions of this view have been defended by Peramatzis (2011), Koslicki (2013: 30–1), and Lowe (2009). Among these interpretations, Peramatzis provides the most thorough and detailed defence of this view. For this reason, my discussion and criticism will concentrate on his defence of the essentialist account.

According to Peramatzis, 'primary substances are prior in substance [= *prior in nature*] to the other entities (that are either said of or in the primary substances), in that insofar as they are subjects of a certain type, particular substances can be without derivative entities, but the converse is not the case.'[111] Peramatzis suggests that both non-substance attributes – such as walking and being white – and non-substance compounds – such as what is walking or the walking thing – are not separate from substances because attributes essentially depend upon a subject (Peramatzis, 2011: 232). By contrast, subjects do not essentially depend upon attributes. Importantly, Peramatzis restricts the relata of the priority relation. According to his reading, primary substances are only prior to non-substance attributes and accidental compounds, but not to essences (secondary substances).[112]

Peramatzis argues that it is an advantage of his reading that it allows us to interpret Aristotle as using the same account of priority in nature in the case of *Metaph.* V 11, VII 1 and *Cat.* 5.[113] He thereby avoids the position that Aristotle uses the term 'priority in nature' equivocally (Peramatzis, 2011: 233).

Peramatzis convincingly argues that the discussion about the primacy of primary substances is closely connected to the discussion about the subjecthood of primary substances. This is an appealing feature of his reading. However, the way in which Peramatzis makes this connection is problematic. His reading of the conditional formulation ('If the primary substances were not, it would be impossible for any of the other items to be') is unsatisfactory for two independent reasons.

(1) According to Peramatzis' interpretation, the conditional interpretation reads as follows:

> If the primary substances were not what they are, it would be impossible for any of the other items to be what they are, but if the other items were not what they are, it would be possible for the primary substances to be what they are.

Peramatzis' reading is problematic as a result of his understanding of the word '*einai*' in this passage. It is true that '*einai*' has a complete use (best understood as 'to exist') and an incomplete use (a predicative use, whereby '*einai*' functions only as a copula) (Brown, 1994). Yet Peramatzis' use of the predicative reading is too liberal. In particular, his assumption that one can just add 'what it is' after any occurrence of '*einai*' is not justified, especially since he does not tell us anything about the principles that would legitimate such an addition.

---

[111] Peramatzis (2011: 231). Cf. Peramatzis (2011: 230-2).

[112] According to Peramatzis, Aristotle makes the same point in *Metaph.* VII 1, where he claims that primary substances are the only beings that can exist separately.

[113] *Metaph.* V 11, 1019a5–6; VII 1, 1028a31–4.

There should be restrictions on the predicative reading. For instance, one should only be allowed to add a predicate to '*einai*' where the context clearly demands it. However, in this case we have no legitimate reason to add the predicate 'what it is' to '*einai*'. Moreover, 'what it is' is not just any predicate; rather it has a definite use within the technical vocabulary of the *Categories*. Hence, further restrictions should apply.

(2) The success of Peramatzis' interpretation depends to a large extent on whether he is able to show that Aristotle uses only one account of priority in nature. The aim of showing that Aristotle uses a univocal account of priority in nature is what drives his whole project as developed in his extensive monograph on the topic. Peramatzis argues that in the *Metaphysics* Aristotle thinks that priority in nature is an asymmetric essential dependence. Peramatzis claims that if his essentialist interpretation of this passage in the *Categories* were correct, this would unify the discussion of priority in nature in the *Categories* with the discussion of priority in nature in the *Metaphysics*.

In my view, his claim that Aristotle argues in the *Metaphysics* that priority in nature is asymmetric essential dependence is not convincing, but I cannot argue for this view within the scope of the present section.[114] However, even disregarding the question of whether Aristotle uses a univocal account of priority in nature in the *Metaphysics* and the *Categories*, it is questionable whether Peramatzis is in a position to submit a unified reading of priority in nature even within the *Categories*. For Peramatzis himself acknowledges that Aristotle uses an existential account of priority in nature in *Cat.* 12. 'Aristotle's example of priority as "non-reciprocation in implication of being" is fairly straightforward. He holds that the unit is prior in this way to the number two in that, if two is, necessarily the unit is. But if the unit is, it is not necessary that two is' (Peramatzis, 2011: 234–5). Now, Peramatzis argues that primary substances cannot be prior in this way to non-substance attributes and compounds:

> Clearly, though, if this is the way in which particular substances are intended to be primary, it is extremely difficult to derive the correct results. For, if Socrates is, necessarily the species man and the genus animal are. However, if either the species man or the genus animal is, it is not necessary that Socrates is. Moreover, because the species necessarily implies the genus, it turns out that genera are prior to species in this sense. But this gets the priority relations introduced in the *Categories* completely the wrong way around. Not only do species and genera, the secondary substances of the *Categories*, prove prior to Aristotle's primary, particular substances. Even within the class of secondary substances it is not the species but the genus that

---

[114] For a criticism of Peramatzis' view, see Malink (2013).

seems to be primary. Aristotle's considered view, however, is that species are (secondary) substances 'more' or 'rather than', and so are prior to, genera (2b7–14; 17–22; 29–34). (Peramatzis, 2011: 235.)

Strikingly, Peramatzis does not mention Aristotle's discussion of the priority of the genus over the species in *Cat.* 13:

> Genera, however, are always prior [sc. in nature] to species since they do not reciprocate as to implication of being; e.g. if there is a fish, then there is an animal, but if there is an animal then there is not necessarily a fish. (*Cat.* 13, 15a4–7.)

The ontological priority between the genus animal and the species fish arguably consists in an asymmetric existential dependence among the instances of the genus and the species:

> Necessarily, if a fish exists, an animal exists, but not necessarily, if an animal exists, a fish exists.

Even though we have seen that the existential-instances reading runs into difficulties (due to the fact that according to Aristotle it is necessary that there is something which is a fish), this passage is most naturally read as invoking an asymmetric existential dependence – accordingly, this passage suggests that Aristotle does not have a univocal account of ontological priority in terms of asymmetric *essential* dependence.

On the face of it, the essentialist reading of priority in nature makes sense. Aristotle says that the genus is prior in nature to the species (*Cat.* 13, 15a4–7) and the genus is essentially prior to the species. However, the essential dependence does not capture the priority in nature as Aristotle develops it here. When Aristotle explains the priority of the genus over the species, he does not say that the genus is prior to the species because the genus makes the species what it is. Rather he speaks about asymmetric ontological implication (= implication of being). On the essentialist reading (reading '*einai*' as 'being what it is' in the conditional), the passage reads as follows:

> If fish is what it is, then animal is what it is, but, not necessarily, if animal is what it is, fish is what it is.

The essentialist reading of '*einai*' in this passages is not plausible.

Peramatzis is certainly right in pointing out that there are other passages in which Aristotle argues for the priority of the species over the genus (*Cat.* 2b7–14, 17–22, and 29–34). In these passages, Aristotle says that the species is prior to the genus because the species is 'more informative' than the genus (they reveal to a greater degree the primary substances of which they are predicated) and because the species is a subject for the genus. Evidently, Aristotle uses a different account for the priority of the species in this passage. The discussion is clearly different from the discussion of the priority of the genus. The most straightforward reading is that Aristotle talks about different understandings of priority in these passages. Peramatzis neglects the passages in which Aristotle establishes the priority in nature of the genus over the species in terms of an existential independence. This is unsatisfactory. Thus we end up with at least two different accounts of priority in nature even on Peramatzis' interpretation. Peramatzis' claim that he can put forward a unified account of priority in nature even within the *Categories* is, thus, called into question.

4.6 Interpreting *Categories* 5, 2b3–6 in Its Context

In this subsection I argue that in contrast to the asymmetric readings, the neutral reading offers an interesting account without running into major interpretative difficulties. If we read *Cat.* 5, 2b3–6 carefully in its context, we see that Aristotle makes an inference in this passage. There he claims that an existential dependence of secondary substances, accidental particulars, and accidental universals *follows from* the fact that the primary substances are their subjects or hosts.[115] Just before 2b3–6 Aristotle explains that:

> All the other things are either said of the primary substances as subjects or in them as subjects. This is clear from an examination of cases. For example, animal is predicated of man and therefore also of the individual man; for were it predicated of none of the individual men it would not be predicated of man at all. Again, colour is in body and therefore also in an individual body; for were it not in some individual body it would not be in body at all. Thus all the other things are either said of the primary substances as subjects or in them as subjects. *So* if the primary substances were not, it would be impossible for any of the other things to be. (*Cat.* 5, 2a24–2b6; transl. Ackrill, 1963, my italics.)

The way in which Aristotle introduces the conditional formulation ('if the primary substances were not …'), namely with a 'so' (*oun*), suggests that he is drawing a consequence from the previous discussion.[116] The conditional holds because the primary substances are subjects or hosts for the other items.

---

[115] I am reading '*einai*' and '*ousôn*' as meaning 'to exist'. The essentialist interpretation is somewhat forced. The more natural reading is the existential reading, and that is the reading I will follow here.

[116] See my remarks on the dittography in 2bc.

Secondary substances, accidental particulars, and accidental universals existentially depend upon primary substances because they are either in them or predicated of them.[117] Note that this does not mean that their primacy consists in this existential dependence. Aristotle does not identify being primary with the existential dependence relation. Rather the 'being a subject for all other items' merely explains why there is an existential dependence of all other items on the primary substances. If we read Aristotle as making a claim only about the dependence of secondary substances and items in other categories on the primary substances, then we can easily account for the inference that he explicitly draws.[118]

We can still understand the relevance of and motivation behind the discussion, even if we read Aristotle as stating a dependence of the secondary substances and items in other categories on the primary substances. Even this limited dependence claim is striking in the philosophical environment of Plato's Academy. It is the first formulation of *in re* universals in the history of philosophy. Plato defends the existence of *ante rem* universals, i.e. universals that can exist even if there are no primary substances taken collectively. He would not at all agree with Aristotle that the secondary substances or accidental universals existentially depend upon the primary substances, given the kinds of items that Aristotle claims primary substances to be, i.e. ordinary objects such as Socrates, Perry the donkey, etc.[119]

According to Plato's metaphysical theory, the conditional 'So if the primary substances were not, it would be impossible for any of the other things to be' is false. He might agree that the primary substances are subjects of predication for universals, but he would reject the view that this will have an impact on the ontological independence of the universals. Whether or not they are

---

[117] Duerlinger (1970) provides a detailed account of how Aristotle uses different senses of 'being in' and 'being predicated of' in order to argue for the existential dependence of secondary substances, accidental particulars, and accidental universals on the primary substances. I concur with Duerlinger's analysis of these notions. Because Duerlinger provides such an extensive discussion, I will limit my own discussion of this issue to the central points.

[118] Aristotle mainly argues in 2a24–2b6 for the view that the primary substances are subjects for all other items, rather than for the view that the other items existentially depend upon them. This reading is supported by the fact that in 2b3–5 he repeats the claim with which the argument began ('All the other things are either said of the primary substances as subjects or in them as subjects,' 2a34–5). The typical organisation of an Aristotelian paragraph is as follows: Aristotle initially states his claim, he argues for it, and he repeats his claim again at the end. We can also find this typical organisation in 2a24–2b6. The fact that he is repeating the same lines shows that he is stressing this point, namely that the primary substances are subjects for all other items. When he speaks about the idea that all other items existentially depend upon them, he draws a further consequence. But he is primarily interested in their being subjects and hosts. On the traditional reading, he is focusing on the dependence claim.

[119] Cf. Duerlinger (1970: 198 and 201).

predicated of something, the universals, i.e. the Platonic forms, exist on their own.[120] Aristotle is attacking this assumption of Plato by claiming that the secondary substances and beings in other categories existentially depend upon the primary substances. This is a huge step for someone who himself has been raised in the Academy.

In sum, these considerations suggest that Aristotle's claim that secondary substances and items in other categories depend upon primary substances makes perfectly good sense and is highly interesting and challenging in the philosophical context in which Aristotle is writing.

4.7 The Primacy of Primary Substances

In the *Categories* Aristotle says that particular objects, for example, Socrates and Plato, are *primary* substances.[121] How does he establish the primacy of particular substances in the *Categories*? So far most interpreters have claimed that he establishes the primacy of the primary substances on the basis of the conditional formulation in *Cat.* 5, 2b3–6. They have claimed that Aristotle's formulation is equivalent to the formulation of priority in nature that he provides in other passages in the *Categories*, for instance in chapters 7, 12, and 13, and in other places in the *Metaphysics*, for instance in V 11.[122] I will now argue that this view is mistaken because these commentators are confusing the primacy of primary substances with a priority in nature relation.

In several passages in the *Categories* in which Aristotle mentions the primacy of primary substances, he states that their primacy consists in the fact that they are subjects for all other beings:

> A substance – that which is called a substance most strictly (*kuriôtata*), primarily (*prôtôs*), and most of all (*malista*) – is that which is neither said of a subject nor in a subject, e.g. the individual man or the individual horse. (*Cat.* 5, 2a11–14; transl. Ackrill, 1963.)

> Further, it is because the primary substances are subjects for all the other things and all the other things are predicated of them or are in them, that they

---

[120] Duerlinger (1970: 182) convincingly argues that Aristotle introduces the distinction between predication and inherence in the *Categories* in order to specify different ways in which universals depend upon the primary substances. This helps him to argue against Plato's view that forms are existentially independent from particulars.

[121] By contrast, in the *Metaphysics* Aristotle says that primary substances are essences or substantial forms and that only in virtue of these substantial forms are hylomorphic compounds (= particular objects) called substances (*Metaph.* VII 11, 1037a27–30). He repeats the claim that particular objects are substances in *Metaph.* VIII 1, 1042a24–31.

[122] *Cat.* 7, 7b15–8a12; 12, 14a29–35; 13, 14b24–15a12. *Metaph.* 1019a4–6.

are called substances most of all (*malista ousiai legontai*). (*Cat.* 5, 2b15–17;
transl. Ackrill, 1963.)

In 2b15–17 Aristotle says explicitly that a primary substance is neither in
another item nor said of other items.[123] I assume that he uses the notions 'most
strictly', 'most of all', and 'primary' in 2b15–17 and 2a11–15 interchangeably. 'Being a primary substance' just means 'being a substance in the strictest
sense'. They are primary because every predication must start with them and
they are not predicated of anything else, nor are they in anything, as Aristotle
states in 2a11–15. They have no subject prior to them in the line of predication,
and that is why they are first or 'primary'.

The 'primacy' of the primary substances has to be distinguished from 'priority in nature'. The problem of the asymmetrical reading is that it assumes,
without any justification, that they are the same (i.e. it assumes that the reason
why the primary substances are called 'primary' is that they are *prior in nature*
to other items). As we have seen in the previous sections, in several passages in
the *Categories* Aristotle theorises about priority in nature.[124] In almost all passages priority in nature is understood as an asymmetric existential dependence
relation. By contrast, Aristotle most probably says that the primacy of primary
substances consists in their being subjects or hosts for all other items. 'Being
a subject' is different from 'being asymmetrically capable of existing without
another item'. The concepts of 'being primary' and 'being prior in nature', as
Aristotle uses them here in the *Categories*, are, thus, different.

In contrast to other interpretations, on my reading, 'being primary' does not
entail 'being prior'. The fact that A is a subject or host for B does not entail
that there is an asymmetrical existential dependence relation between A and
B (which would mean that A can exist without B, but not conversely). We
need additional information as to why we should think that A could indeed
exist without B. Aristotle does not provide us with any such information,
probably because he does not hold the view that the primary substances are
in any way ontologically independent from secondary substances or items
in the other categories. This would indeed be a philosophically challenging
position to defend, because one would need to defend the possibility of the
existence of bare substrata. So I take it that, in this regard too, my view is
preferable to other interpretations, because it offers a closer and more careful
reading of the text and attributes to Aristotle less implausible philosophical
views.

---

[123] Cf. *Cat.* 2, 1b3–6.
[124] *Cat.* 7, 7b15–8a12; 12, 14a29–35; 13, 14b24–15a12.

The following concern might be raised in response to my suggestion that we explain the primacy of the primary substances in terms of their subjecthood. One does not offer an account of the primacy by claiming that their primacy consists in their being subjects. On this reading, Aristotle merely makes claims about primacy without offering any justification for it. Compare the discussion in *Metaph.* III 3, 998a20–b14, in which he questions whether the highest genera or the constitutive elements of an entity have better claims to be the first principles. It would be rather uninformative to merely claim that one or the other has a better claim to it without providing any justification for why this should be so.

Interpreters who claim that, according to Aristotle, the primacy of the primary substances just consists in their being subjects, ascribe to Aristotle precisely this move, namely to simply make claims about primacy without providing independent reasons for why exactly 'being a subject' should account for primacy. In *Metaph.* III 3, 998a20–b14 one can see, though, that Aristotle is aware of these kinds of concerns and that he does not simply take subjecthood to be a criterion or condition for priority.[125]

This concern is a reasonable one. Yet I think that it is no less problematic than the view it criticises. It is certainly right to point out that on my reading Aristotle would not offer a justification for why subjecthood should account for primacy. However, I find it problematic to use his discussions in the *Metaphysics* as a proof against my reading. In this Element I have tried to keep the discussions in the *Categories* separate from those in the *Metaphysics*. This is methodological, since I find it problematic to read the discussions in the *Metaphysics*, which are often more developed, into the *Categories*. For a reader who only knows the *Categories*, the subjecthood criterion is the best criterion for substancehood and primacy. Only later in the *Metaphysics*, especially *Metaph.* III and VII 3, does Aristotle seem to seriously question the adequacy of the subjecthood criterion. Thus, rather than reading the *Metaphysics* into the *Categories*, I suggest that we could read the discussions in the *Metaphysics* as answers to criticisms that Aristotle might have encountered as a result of his treatment of primary substances in the *Categories*.

In light of these observations, I find it rather problematic to ascribe to Aristotle an asymmetrical ontological dependence claim when he only explicitly makes claims about the dependence of the secondary substances and items

---

[125] Note that although this move seems unsatisfactory, some interpreters have claimed that as regards what is basic, it might just be decided by intuitions whether one follows Aristotle or Plato. On this view, the controversy simply does not have a determinate answer. See Fine (1993).

in other categories on the primary substances. Thus the more careful view is that Aristotle says that the other beings cannot exist without the primary substances, but that he does not implicitly claim that the primary substances can exist without the other beings.

4.8 Conclusion

In this section, I have defended a neutral reading of *Cat.* 5, 2b3–6 and argued that, in the passage under discussion, Aristotle commits himself only to the view that items in other categories and secondary substances existentially depend upon primary substances, and he does not also commit himself to the view that primary substances do not existentially depend upon secondary substances and items in other categories. I have raised problems for alternative interpretations, showing that the debate is unduly complicated by a pervasive but ultimately dubious assumption: namely, that Aristotle appeals here to an asymmetric ontological relationship between primary substances and secondary substances and items in other categories. I have contended that Aristotle does not establish the primacy of primary substances in terms of an asymmetric dependence relation. Rather, he says that their primacy consists in their being subjects and hosts for secondary substances, accidental universals, and accidental particulars. The reading I defend is both closer to the text and more charitable, because it does not ascribe to Aristotle any implausible views about the ontological status of primary substances. It is my view that Aristotle's claims in this passage are intelligible, interesting, and, considering the philosophical context of his writing, highly challenging.

5 Conclusion

In this Element, I have analysed Aristotle's account of ontological priority (what he calls 'priority in substance' (*proteron kata ousian*) or 'priority in nature' (*proteron tēi phusei*)), which he conceives of as asymmetric ontological dependence between two *beings* (*onta*). In offering a detailed reconstruction of the passages on ontological priority in the *Categories*, I hope to have demonstrated that Aristotle's theory on ontological priority, while problematic, is more profound and more sophisticated than previously thought. Aristotle's discussion of ontological priority incorporates concepts with which philosophers still engage today. Moreover, he has a theoretical background, which might be conducive to further integrating his findings into current discussions on ontological priority, in particular his discussions on simultaneity in nature, on essences (both reciprocal and non-reciprocal), on implication, and on counterpossibles.

Until now, two understandings of Aristotle's account of ontological dependence have been predominant: one in terms of asymmetric existential dependence and the other in terms of asymmetric essential dependence. My reading shows that the debate about whether Aristotle has a modal-existential or an essentialist account of priority has been based on a mistaken presupposition, namely that Aristotle employs '*einai*' univocally. By showing that within a single statement on ontological priority and simultaneity Aristotle often uses the notion '*einai*' in different ways, I have shown that no unified account is adequate.

My reading provides a less unified picture of Aristotle's account of ontological priority than previous readings. Although it is somewhat unsatisfactory to not have a unified account, my reading is closer to the text and establishes its results on a broader textual basis than previous interpretations that attempt to develop a unified reading. In particular, I have argued for a disjunctive account consisting of the following two sufficient conditions that are disjunctively necessary:

(1) A is ontologically prior to B if necessarily B's being implies A's being, but not necessarily, A's being implies B's being.

(2) A is ontologically prior to B if necessarily A's being implies B's being, and necessarily, B's being implies A's being; and A's being is a cause of B's being.

I have argued that 'implication of being' can be understood either existentially or predicatively (whereby I subsume the veridical reading under the predicative reading), and that we even have 'mixed' readings (in which case two different uses of '*einai*' are employed in the same statement about priority). How one is to read the 'implication of being' must be decided on a case-by-case basis. I argued that in none of the relevant passages on ontological priority does Aristotle use '*einai*' in the sense of 'what it is', as is claimed by defenders of the essentialist reading of ontological priority.

Although it would be preferable to develop a unified account of ontological priority (for instance, the two criteria could be considered to be expressions of an underlying account of ontological priority in terms of an asymmetric essentialist dependence relation), such a reading faces significant difficulties. Why would Aristotle never explicitly state the unified account? He could have easily done so. Instead he repeatedly returns to the traditional Academic formulation of ontological priority in terms of asymmetric implication of being (with its various formulations).

In my reconstruction, Aristotle's theory of ontological priority still exhibits some serious shortcomings, since it cannot establish priorities in cases of necessary existents and makes everything ontologically dependent upon them. In brief, it runs into many, if not all, of the problems that have been raised against the existentialist account – in addition to the above-mentioned problems of unity. Yet although Aristotle implicitly anticipates worries about the conditional analysis of ontological dependence in existential terms in his discussion of hypothetical necessity (*Gen. corr.* 337b14–337b24), he does not put into practice many useful tools that are available to him. What I find deeply puzzling about Aristotle's treatment of ontological priority is that although he has the resources to avoid many of these problems (by distinguishing, for instance, between various kinds of implication, or by grounding the relevant implications in the essences of the relata), Aristotle does not make use of them. Moreover, I have shown that his discussion of ontological priority concerning relatives is fraught with difficulties, though the relevant problems do not derive from his account of ontological priority but from problems internal to his theory of relatives.

I have argued that the notion of ontological priority plays a less central role in the *Categories* than one would have expected. In particular, I have argued that the primacy of the primary substances does not consist in their ontological priority over secondary substances and items in other categories. Rather, their primacy consists in their being subjects for other items. This finding is striking, since one would most naturally suppose that their primacy would consist in an ontological priority, given that Aristotle ascribes to them the most prominent role in his ontology in the *Categories*.

This study has notable implications for our understanding of discussions of priority within the Academy. If I am right, then there is a greater continuity within the Academy than hitherto recognised. Although Aristotle further develops Plato's account of ontological priority in terms of non-reciprocal implication of being, Aristotle nevertheless remains a faithful pupil of Plato. What is more, discussions within the Academy on which beings are fundamental can be seen in a new light: rather than arguing about what constitute the best criteria for ontological priority, they seem to largely agree on this point and primarily argue as to what best satisfies these criteria. This important aspect is absent from existing scholarship, and in drawing attention to it here, my reading offers new insights into the metaphysical investigations conducted in the Academy.

The same structure and the same ambiguous use of '*einai*' are evident already in Plato's formulations of priority (if we can trust Aristotle's testimony). The question is whether Plato or Aristotle would have seen a real difference. Taking up the suggestions of earlier studies on the use of '*einai*' in Ancient philosophy, my reading supports the view that both philosophers see no clear-cut semantic distinctions. In this light, one can at least explain why they so easily switch from one use to the other. I have argued that if they do draw a distinction between the predicative and the existential reading, the existential reading would nevertheless follow from the predicative reading in most cases, given that the terms with which Aristotle operates in his scientific writings are not empty.

Whilst agreeing with his predecessors in a number of respects, I have shown that Aristotle has added a further sufficient condition for ontological priority in the form of mutual implication of being, where one relatum is the cause of the other relatum. Moreover, I have argued that Aristotle advanced the Academic discussions on ontological priority by explicitly using modal operators in his conditions for priority and also, arguably, by implicitly using temporal operators.

The findings of the present study should be useful in helping us to understand better the *Metaphysics*. Since the notion of priority in substance is closely connected to many important notions – such as 'substance' and 'separation' – understanding his discussion of priority in substance yields important insights into his metaphysical project. Let me bring the study to a close by noting a few specific findings that will contribute to this end.

Also in the *Metaphysics* Aristotle theorises about criteria for ontological priority and puts them into use in a number of places.[126] The main passages where Aristotle discusses ontological priority are *Metaph.* V 11 and IX 8. In addition to these two passages, Aristotle employs his notion of priority (without theorising about it) in *Metaph.* XII 6. The relata of an ontological priority relation in the *Metaphysics* are manifold: (1) form and matter (*Metaph.* VII, 1019a4–14; (2) parts and wholes (*Metaph.* VII, 1019a4–14; (3) numbers (*Metaph.* XIII 8, 1083b–33); (4) relatives (*Metaph.* IV, 1010b30–1011a2); (5) primary substances and accidents (*Metaph.* VII, 1019a4–14; VII 1, 1028a10–b1); (6) capacities and activities (*Metaph.* III 6, 1002b32–1003a5; IX 8 1050a4–1050b6; IX 8, 1050b6–28; XII 6, 1071b22-1072a4); (7) eternal substances and perishable substances (*Metaph.* III 6, 1002b32–1003a5; IX 8, 1050b6–28; XII 6, 1071b22–1072a4). Aristotle already considered some of these cases in the *Categories* (numbers, primary substances and accidents, relatives), whereas some

---

[126] Interestingly, although simultaneity in nature takes up considerable space in the rather brief *Categories*, Aristotle does not offer a discussion on simultaneity in nature in the *Metaphysics*.

of the relata are new. This should not be surprising, given that some of the relata are first introduced in the *Metaphysics* as new entities of reality (form and matter, capacities and activities, eternal and perishable substances).

Whilst it is widely held that Aristotle has a univocal account of ontological priority in the *Categories* and in the *Metaphysics*, be it in terms of either existence (Kirwan (1993); Witt (1994); Makin (2003)) or essences,[127] I think that Aristotle has a pluralistic account of ontological priority in the *Categories* and in the *Metaphysics*.[128] To the disjunctive account of ontological priority that we find in the *Categories*, he adds a new so-called 'teleological' criterion as a further sufficient condition for ontological priority. According to this criterion, if A and B are both items or stages of a teleologically structured process, then A is prior in substance to B, if A is posterior in this process (i.e. if A occurs after B has already occurred). Moreover, whilst he explicitly continues to use in the *Metaphysics* a specific part of the account of ontological priority from the *Categories*, namely asymmetric implication of being (and its logically equivalent formulations), he does not expressly mention the second sufficient condition for ontological priority – namely symmetrical implication of being – where one of the items is the cause of the other item.[129]

I hope to show in my future research that Aristotle is primarily interested in ontological priority because he wishes to establish the absolute ontological priority of the unmoved movers.

---

[127] Peramatzis (2011). The evidence from the *Categories* puts significant pressure on essentialist readings of the *Metaphysics*, since it shows decisively that Aristotle does construe ontological priority in existential terms in some cases. If Peramatzis' interpretation of the *Metaphysics* were right, one would expect Aristotle to distance himself from his previous understanding of ontological priority, all the more so since – as I hope to have shown – such a view was not unique to him, but rather was something he shared with other thinkers from the Academy.

[128] The view that Aristotle has a pluralistic account of ontological priority is not new (see Panayides (1999) and Beere (2009)). However, my take on it differs from that of previous interpreters in that I argue that the different sufficient conditions for ontological priority do not differ in terms of their domains of application.

[129] It is debatable whether or not he employs it implicitly in some cases. Some scholars contend that he does implicitly use it in *Metaph.* XII 6, 1071b22–1072a4. See Menn (2009) and Frey (2015).

References

Ackrill, J. L. (1957). Plato and the Copula: Sophist 251–259. *The Journal of Hellenic Studies*, **77**, 1–6.

(1963). *Aristotle's Categories and De Interpretatione: Translated with Notes*, Oxford: Clarendon.

Aristotle and Lorenzo Minio-Paluello. (1956). *Aristotelis Categoriae et Liber de interpretatione*, Oxford: Clarendon.

Aristotle and J. A. Smith. (1931). De Anima. Oxford: Clarendon.

Barnes, J. L. (2007). *Truth, Etc.*, Oxford: Oxford University Press.

Beere, Jonathan B. (2009). *Doing and Being: An Interpretation of Aristotle's Metaphysics Theta*, Oxford: Oxford University Press.

Bjerring, Jens Christian. (2014). On counterpossibles. *Philosophical Studies*, **168**, 327–53.

Bobzien, Susanne. (2000). Wholly hypothetical syllogisms. *Phronesis*, **45**, 87–137.

Bodéüs, Richard and Annick Stevens. (2014). *Aristote, Métaphysique Livre Delta*, Paris: Vrin.

Bostock, D. (2006). Aristotle on teleology in nature. In *Space, Time, Matter, and Form: Essays on Aristotle's Physics*, Oxford: Oxford University Press, 48–78.

Brown, L. (1994). The verb *to be* in Greek philosophy. In S. Everson, ed., *Language*, Cambridge: Cambridge University Press, 212–36.

Cleary, John J. (1988). *Aristotle on the Many Senses of Priority*, Carbondale: Southern Illinois University Press.

Coope, Ursula. (2005). *Time for Aristotle: Physics IV*, Oxford: Oxford University Press.

Corkum, Phil. (2008). Aristotle on ontological dependence. *Phronesis*, **53**, 65–92.

(2016). Ontological dependence and grounding in Aristotle. *Oxford HandElements Online*. Retrieved 18 July 2017 from www.oxfordhand Elements.com/view/10.1093/oxfordhb/9780199935314.001.0001/oxford hb-9780199935314-e-31.

Correia, Fabrice. (2008). Ontological dependence. *Philosophy Compass*, **3**(5), 1013–32.

Crivelli, Paolo. (2004). *Aristotle on Truth*, Cambridge: Cambridge University Press.

Duerlinger, James. (1970). Predication and inherence in Aristotle's *Categories*. *Phronesis*, **15**(2), 179–203.

Duncombe, Matthew. (2015). Aristotle's two accounts of relatives in *Categories* 7. *Phronesis*, **60**(4): 436–61.

(2020). *Ancient Relativity: Plato, Aristotle, Stoics, and Sceptics*, Oxford: Oxford University Press.

Ebrey, David. (2015). Why are there no conditionals in Aristotle's logic? *Journal of the History of Philosophy*, **53**(2), 185–205.

Fine, Gail. (1993). *On Ideas*, Oxford: Clarendon.

Fine, Kit. (1994a). Essence and modality. *Philosophical Perspectives*, **8**, 1–16.

(1994b). Senses of essence. In W. Sinnott-Armstrong, D. Raffman, and N. Asher, eds., *Modality, Morality and Belief: Essays in Honor of Ruth Barcan Marcus*, Cambridge: Cambridge University Press, 53–73.

(1995). Ontological dependence. *Proceedings of the Aristotelian Society*, **95**, 269–90.

(2001). Question of realism. *Philosopher's Imprint*, **1**, 1–30.

(1981). Categories in Aristotle. In D. O'Meara, ed., *Studies in Aristotle*, Washington, DC: Catholic University of America Press, 1–24.

Frede, Michael. (1987). Individuals in Aristotle. In M. Frede, ed., *Essays in Ancient Philosophy*, Oxford: Oxford University Press, 49–71.

Frey, Christopher. (2015). Capacities and the eternal in *Metaphysics* Θ.8 and *De Caelo*, *Phronesis*, **60**(1), 88–126.

Gottlieb, Paula. (1993). Aristotle versus Protagoras on relatives and the objects of perception. *Oxford Studies in Ancient Philosophy*, **11**, 101–19.

Hood, Pamela Michelle. (2004). *Aristotle on the Category of Relation*, Lanham: University of America.

Kahn, C. H. (1966). The Greek verb 'to be' and the concept of being. *Foundations of Language*, **2**(3), 245–65.

Kirwan, C. (1993). *Aristotle's* Metaphysics: *Elements Gamma, Delta, and Epsilon*, Oxford: Oxford University Press.

Kohl, Markus. (2008). Substancehood and subjecthood in Aristotle's *Categories*. *Phronesis*, **53**(2), 152–79.

(2012). Varieties of ontological dependence. In F. Correia and B. Schnieder, eds., *Metaphysical Grounding: Understanding the Structure of Reality*, Cambridge: Cambridge University Press, 186–213.

Koslicki, Kathrin. (2013). Ontological dependence: an opinionated survey. In B. Schnieder and A. Steinberg, eds., *Dependence, Emergence, Supervenience*, Munich: Philosophia, 1–34.

Lederman, Harvey. (2014). *ho pote on esti* and coupled entities: a form of explanation in Aristotle's natural philosophy. *Oxford Studies in Ancient Philosophy*, **46**, 109–64.

Loux, Michael J. (1991). *Primary Ousia: An Essay on Aristotle's* Metaphysics Z *and* H, Ithaca: Cornell University Press.

Lowe, E. Jonathan. (2009). Ontological dependence. plato.stanford.edu/ archives/ spr2010/entries/dependence-ontological/

(2003). What does Aristotle mean by priority in substance? *Oxford Studies in Ancient Philosophy*, **24**, 209–38.

Makin, Stephen. (2006). *Aristotle: Metaphysics Theta: Translated with an Introduction and Commentary*, Oxford: Clarendon.

Malcolm, J. (1981). On the generation and corruption of the *categories*. *The Review of Metaphysics*, **34**(4), 662–81.

Malink, Marko. (2013). Essence and being: a discussion of Michail Peramatzis, *Priority in Aristotle's Metaphysics*. *Oxford Studies in Ancient Philosophy*, **45**, 341–60.

Martin, Christopher J. (1999). Non-reductive arguments from impossible hypotheses in Boethius and Philoponus. *Oxford Studies in Ancient Philosophy*, **17**, 279–302.

Menn, Stephen. (2009). *Aporiai* 13–14. In M. Crubellier and A. Laks, eds., *Aristotle:* Metaphysics *Beta*, Oxford: Oxford University Press, 211–66.

Minio-Paluello, L. (1956 [1949]). *Aristotelis Categoriae et Liber de Interpretatione*, Oxford: Clarendon.

Morales, Fabio. (1994). Relational attributes in Aristotle. *Phronesis*, **39**(3), 255–74.

Moravcsik, Julius M. E. (1965). Strawson and ontological priority, *Analytic Philosophy*, 2nd Series, R. J. Butler, ed., Blackwell: Oxford.

(1967). Predication in Aristotle. *Philosophical Review*, **76**(1), 80–96.

Morison, Benjamin. (2011). What was Aristotle's concept of logical form? In B. Morison and K. Ierodiakonou, eds., *Episteme, etc.: Essays in Honour of Jonathan Barnes*, Oxford: Oxford University Press, 172–88.

Mutschmann, Hermann. (1907). *Divisiones quae vulgo dicuntur Aristoteleae*, Leipzig: Teubner.

Owen, G. E. L. (1965). Inherence. *Phronesis*, **10**(1), 97–105.

Panayides, C. (1999). Aristotle on the priority of actuality in substance. *Ancient Philosophy*, **19**, 327–44.

Peramatzis, Michail. (2011). *Priority in Aristotle's Metaphysics*, Oxford: Oxford University Press.

Pines, Shlomo. (1961). A new fragment of Xenocrates and its implications. *Transactions of the American Philosophical Society*, New Series, **51**(2), 3–34.

Quine, Willard V. O. (1963). On what there is. In *From a Logical Point of View*, New York: Harper & Row, 1–19.

Rashed, Marwan. (2004). Priorité de l'eidos ou du genos entre Andronicos et Alexandre: Vestiges Arabes et Grecs Inédits. *Arabis Sciences and Philosophy*, **14**, 9–63.

Roberts, W. Rhys. (2004). *Aristotle: Rhetoric*, Mineola, NY : Dover.

Ross, William David. (1924). *Aristotle's* Metaphysics: *Text and Commentary*, 2 vols., Oxford: Clarendon.

Schaffer, Jonathan. (2009). On what grounds what. In D. Manley, D. J. Chalmers, and R. Wasserman, eds., *Metametaphysics: New Essays on the Foundations of Ontology*, Oxford: Oxford University Press, 347–83.

Sedley, David. (2002). Aristotelian relativities. In M. Canto-Sperber and P. Pellegrin, eds., *Le Style de La Pensée: Receuil de Textes En Hommage À Jacques Brunschwig*, Paris: Les Belles Lettres, 324–52.

Sider, Theodore. (2006). Bare particulars. *Philosophical Perspectives*, **20**, 387–97.

Simons, Peter. (1991). Part/whole II: mereology since 1900. In H. Burkhardt and B. Smith, eds., *HandElement of Metaphysics and Ontology*, Munich: Philosophia, 672–5.

Smith, Robin. (2017). Aristotle's logic. In *The Stanford Encyclopedia of Philosophy* (Spring 2017 edition), Edward N. Zalta, ed., plato.stanford. edu/archives/spr2017/entries/aristotle-logic/.

Smyth, H. W. (1984). *Greek Grammar*, Harvard: Harvard University Press.

Strawson, Peter F. (1959). *Individuals: An Essay in Descriptive Metaphysics*, London: Methuen.

Striker, Gisela. (2011). A note on the ontology in Aristotle's *Categories*, section 2. In B. Morison and K. Ierodiakonou, eds., *Episteme, etc.: Essays in Honour of Jonathan Barnes*, Oxford: Oxford University Press, 141–50.

Studtmann, Paul. (2014). Aristotle's Categories. In *The Stanford Encyclopedia of Philosophy* (Summer 2014 edition), Edward N. Zalta, ed., plato.stanford.edu/archives/sum2014/entries/aristotle-categories/.

Tahko, Tuomas E. and E. Jonathan Lowe. (2020). Ontologial dependence. In *The Stanford Encyclopedia of Philosophy* (Fall 2020 edition), Edward N. Zalta, ed., https://plato.stanford.edu/archives/fall2020/ entries/dependence-ontological.

Tlumak, J. (1983). Cross-categorical priority arguments. *Metaphilosophy*, **14**(1), 32–9.

Vlastos, G. (1981). An ambiguity in the Sophist AS. In G. Vlastos, ed., *Platonic Studies*, Princeton: Princeton University Press, 270–322.

Witt, Charlotte. (1994). The priority of actuality. In T. Scaltsas and D. Charles, eds., *Unity, Identity, and Explanation in Aristotle's* Metaphysics, Oxford: Oxford University Press, 214–28.

Woods, M. J. (1982). *Aristotle's Eudemian Ethics, Elements I, II, and VIII*, Oxford: Clarendon.

Acknowledgements

This Element is the revised version of my dissertation, which was accepted at the Humboldt University of Berlin in June 2018. Many people helped me to write this Element. Most of all I would like to thank my PhD supervisors Jonathan Beere, Ursula Coope, and Marko Malink. Jonathan Beere taught me what it means to be a great teacher and has supported me from the very beginning of this project. Without Ursula Coope's immense support and encouragement during my whole graduate career, this project could not have been completed. Marko Malink's keen insights and acute knowledge of Aristotelian texts made this Element so much better. I received generous financial support for my dissertation project from the Research Training Group Philosophy, Science and the Sciences, the Studienstiftung des deutschen Volkes, and the Fondation Hardt. I would like to thank the chairman of the dissertation committee, Gerd Graßhoff and the external examiner Christoph Helmig. I am grateful to Bettina Bohle, Norbert Blößner, David Charles, Klaus Corcilius, Matthew Duncombe, Paolo Fait, Jim Hankinson, Lindsay Judson, Stephen Menn, Benjamin Morison, Michail Peramatzis, Christian Pfeiffer, Jacob Rosen, and Cecilia Trifogli for many valuable discussions. Audiences in Berlin, Chicago, Hamburg, Köln, London, Luzern, Oxford, Princeton, San Diego, Stockholm, and Uppsala provided useful comments and suggestions. I would like to thank my fellow graduate students in Berlin. The extensive and helpful comments from James Warren as well as an anonymous referee greatly improved this Element. I am grateful to my family for their enduring support. I am indebted to my husband Ralf Bader. There are no words to express my gratitude for the countless ways in which he has supported me. I thank my daughters Charlotte Sophie and Elisabeth Margarethe (who helped me enormously in finalising this project). This Element is dedicated to Ralf.

Cambridge Elements ☰

Ancient Philosophy

James Warren
University of Cambridge

James Warren is Professor of Ancient Philosophy at the University of Cambridge. He is the author of *Epicurus and Democritean Ethics* (Cambridge, 2002), *Facing Death: Epicurus and his Critics* (2004), *Presocratics* (2007), *The Pleasures of Reason in Plato, Aristotle and the Hellenistic Hedonists* (Cambridge, 2014). He is also the editor of *The Cambridge Companion to Epicurus* (Cambridge, 2009), and joint editor of *Authors and Authorities in Ancient Philosophy* (Cambridge, 2018).

About the Series

The Elements in Ancient Philosophy series deals with a wide variety of topics and texts in ancient Greek and Roman philosophy, written by leading scholars in the field. Taking a theme, question, or type of argument, some Elements explore it across antiquity and beyond. Others look in detail at an ancient author, a specific work, or a part of a longer work, considering its structure, content, and significance, or explore more directly ancient perspectives on modern philosophical questions.

Cambridge Elements ≡

Ancient Philosophy

Printed in the United States
By Bookmasters